The Politics of Land Use

R. Robert Linowes
Don T. Allensworth

The Praeger Special Studies program—utilizing the most modern and efficient book production techniques and a selective worldwide distribution network—makes available to the academic, government, and business communities significant, timely research in U.S. and international economic, social, and political development.

The Politics of Land Use

Planning, Zoning, and the Private Developer

Praeger Publishers   New York   Washington   London

PRAEGER SPECIAL STUDIES IN U.S. ECONOMIC, SOCIAL, AND POLITICAL ISSUES

Library of Congress Cataloging in Publication Data

Linowes, R   Robert.
    The politics of land use.

    (Praeger special studies in U.S. economic,
social, and political issues)
    Includes bibliographical references.
    1. Cities and towns—Planning—United States.
2. Zoning—United States. 3. Housing—United
States. I. Allensworth, Donald Trudeau, 1934-
joint author. II. Title.
HT167. L55   309. 2'62'0973   73-8176

PRAEGER PUBLISHERS
111 Fourth Avenue, New York, N.Y. 10003, U.S.A.
5, Cromwell Place, London SW7 2JL, England

Published in the United States of America in 1973
by Praeger Publishers, Inc.

Printed in the United States of America

This study concentrates on a key American problem,
community development. Specifically, it examines planning
and zoning and other land-use policies and practices. A
number of groups participate in the community development
process; one of the most prominent is the private developer.
It is the developer who assembles and prepares land for
private homes, apartments, commercial buildings, and other
uses. And it is the developer or builder who provides the
structures and contributes the basic public improvements
and facilities within subdivisions.

The private developer has gradually become "public
enemy number one." He has been charged with a wide variety
of evil deeds. He is held responsible for the destruction
of the environment, the triggering of urban sprawl, the
indiscriminate leveling of trees, the despoilment of open
spaces, the encroachment on agriculture, and the contamina-
tion of land and water resources.

The developer is also commonly accused of greed,
profit-seeking at public expense, corrupting the political
system for private advantage, and holding the citizenry in
utter contempt. The developer, the reasoning goes, has
ravaged the urban landscape and sought to undermine community planning. It is not too farfetched to suggest that
some people are convinced that he is basically to blame for
the general condition of urban America, which is undis-
putedly beset with a host of physical, social, and economic
problems.

This study argues that urban communities are in the
shape they are in because of public regulations over land
development. The developer is bound by these regulations
and has contributed to our urban ills as a consequence.
The answer, however, is not to pin the blame on developers,
public officials, or others but to get on with the task of
charting directions for the future.

This is precisely the aim of this study: to present
the policies and programs needed to remake our metropolitan
areas. Community planning policy needs to be overhauled,
and zoning policy needs to be significantly restructured.
The greatest emphasis should be placed on zoning, which is
the real power over local development. Communities are
shaped by zoning, and particular zoning patterns will have

enormous effects on the lives, attitudes, political postures, health, and welfare of Americans.

This study seeks to combine the academic and practical perspectives in a field that promises to loom increasingly larger on the urban political horizon. Once relegated to a minor position in college texts on state and local government, planning and zoning now constitute an independent concentration in the nation's leading universities.

The study is a joint effort. Linowes, a widely experienced zoning attorney, provided many of the comments concerning the ideal qualities to be achieved in the urban environment and the general means of attaining them; Allensworth, a political scientist, focused on the impact of these concepts and proposals on the political system and on the prospects of the desired ends being produced by different public powers and particular levels of government. The overall tone of the work as well as the specific observations represent the views and input of both authors.

R. Robert Linowes
Don T. Allensworth

CONTENTS

The Politics of
Land Use

1

INTRODUCTION:
ESSENTIALS OF
URBAN PLANNING

Urban planning is in a transitional state today. This is not unusual, since planning has undergone several changes since its emergence in the colonial days. Urban planning encompasses a wide variety of particulars not readily subject to precise delineation, and its scope is broadening as the years pass. It has been given credit for various accomplishments, and it has been charged with the responsibility for creating a number of problems.

Urban planning has been studied from several different vantage points. F. Stuart Chapin, for instance, approaches the topic from a technical point of view, outlining the techniques of conducting employment, population, transportation, and other planning studies.[1] Donald H. Webster sees urban planning as basically a matter of public administration, concentrating mainly on the municipal bureaucracy and local government powers affecting planning.[2] T. J. Kent tends to view planning in terms of the norms and values that must prevail if planning is to be effective,[3] while Alan Altshuler describes urban planning in the light of the political process.[4]

Urban planning is, of course, of concern to city planning departments in colleges and universities, but it is also of concern to other disciplines. Political scientists, for instance, have developed a keen interest in urban planning,[5] as have sociologists.[6] Furthermore, planning increasingly is being examined through interdisciplinary study, an approach that draws upon a variety of academic fields in quest of behavioral and other relevant knowledge.

Yet planning is not entirely an academic matter. It is an important practical field that includes a large number of administrators, professionals, technicians, and consultants, operating mostly at the municipal level. Both academicians and practitioners help make urban planning what it is. Many others, in addition, have important stakes in the administration of the urban planning function, and these include a wide array of public and private forces. These forces are concerned also with planning and its future.

THE NATURE OF THIS STUDY

This is a study of urban planning and of the various public and private activities that are considered part of or that impact upon the urban planning process. It focuses most attention on urban planning policy and its administration; zoning, a key planning-related power; urban housing policy, which may be shaped by planning; and neighborhood citizens associations, which may exercise significant power over planning, zoning, and housing policies. Other topics discussed include public controls over new subdivisions, the programs of various influential government bureaucracies whose powers help mold urban development patterns, and the role of the business community in the planning process.

The purposes of the study are: (1) to present the picture of urban planning policy and practices as found in America today; (2) to examine the effects of urban planning and the various land-use, housing, and building control policies; (3) to study the problems in urban planning and related policy areas; and (4) to advance alternatives to current planning and urban development policies and practices. The subjects covered are urban planning policy, zoning policy, housing policy, citizens associations, and directions for the future.

Chapter 2 reviews the current state of urban planning, the environment of planning administration and policy-making, the relative degree of success in different types of planning, and the recent history of planning decision-making. It advances suggestions for improving the planning process.

Chapter 3 depicts the vital part that zoning plays in structuring land use and development; the nature of the link between planning and zoning; zoning trends and patterns; the fiscal, economic, and social effects of contemporary zoning practices; and problems with zoning. It considers, generally, the ways in which current practices can be redirected.

Chapter 4 examines the relationship between planning and housing policy; present housing conditions in the

metropolitan area; the various governmental programs and
duties in housing; the politics of housing, building, and
land-use control policies and decision-making; the effects
of public policy on housing; community resistance to low-
income housing; and, broadly, possible means of changing
local policies affecting housing.

Chapter 5 concentrates on the roles, interests, and
political influence of neighborhood citizens associations.
The chapter distinguishes between different kinds of citizens organizations, analyzes the philosophical and practical bases and the policy concerns of citizens associations,
and discusses the implications of citizens associations'
dominance of community planning and land-use politics.

The final chapter, Chapter 6, presents proposals for
the future. It summarizes the key recommendations discussed in Chapters 2 through 5 and examines in a broader,
more detailed, and more systematic sense than in the earlier chapters the changes that can be made to advance the
art of planning. It presents new ideas and recommendations
not found in the earlier chapters. Proposals for restruc-
turing planning and urban development policies, practices,
and processes are based on a careful assessment of the political system and its potential for effecting meaningful
change.

The theme of the study is that planning and zoning
policies all too often have been misdirected, that planning
and zoning powers all too often have been misused. In
legal theory, planning and zoning are powers delegated to
community governments to protect the health, safety, welfare, and morals of the people. In practice, planning and
zoning have had a much narrower aim: the protection of
the single-family residence. Planning and zoning, fortified
by other governmental powers, commonly have been instruments
for the prevention of needed commercial, high-density residential, public facility, and industrial development.

Present planning and urban development policies frequently dictate separation of differing land uses. This
means that residential sections are set off from commercial,
office, shopping, entertainment, public facility, and working sections and that different types of residence are
separated from one another. Current policies often have
had disastrous effects: the community tax base has suffered,
community transportation systems are less efficient, community residents are isolated from shopping and office areas,
the environment is polluted by unnecessary automobile travel,
economic class divisions are encouraged, racial segregation
is virtually assured, economic productivity is lowered, and

the supply of housing for moderate-income families is curtailed.

The book proposes that land uses be mixed and that planning, zoning, and other public policies be used to promote this end. The mixture of land uses adds a dimension of vitality and variety to communities; it serves as a desirable substitute for the bland monotony so typical of much outlying city and suburban development. A single neighborhood should contain a mixture of townhouses, garden apartments, and single-family dwellings. It should include a shopping facility containing a drug store, a grocery, and other desired commercial establishments, within easy walking distance of home. In areas for which more intensive development is appropriate, office buildings could be located alongside higher density apartment houses so that residents could walk to work. The mixture need not be extreme; some separation of land uses should be expected, but diversity should be a major goal.

Mixing land uses can serve to strengthen the community's tax base, reduce building costs, cut the expense of providing public improvements, and widen the potential housing market. Commercial buildings, shopping centers, and apartment houses commonly add more to community tax coffers than they draw out in services. Lower building costs and lower public improvement costs can lead to housing for additional income groups. With basic commercial and business areas near residences, more efficient transportation systems are made possible and automobile pollution is curtailed. Proximity of home to place of work should enhance economic productivity by reducing absenteeism, tardiness, turnover, and fatigue. New policies can mean a better community, and they can provide the citizens and the developers with the incentives to build such a community.

We live in an age of change. So far, the planning and urban development policies of many communities have remained immune from the winds of change. Proposals in this study point the way toward change that can be orderly and constructive. The alternative may be more radical change imposed from outside the community by forces beyond local control and not subject to local influence.

BASIC FEATURES OF PLANNING

Planning, as used in this book, refers to the process of establishing goals, guides, and directions for future community development. Planning covers the physical (land-

use), economic, and social aspects of community development. Traditionally, planning has stressed land use, but
in recent years the field has broadened to encompass the
full range of activities related to community growth and
development. Community planners still tend to focus most
of their attention on land use and physical development.
     The product of the planning process is the master
plan, which may go by different names depending on the community. The conventional master plan includes land-use,
community facilities, and circulation components. The land-
use portion is concerned with private property, the community facilities portion with such matters as schools and
recreation areas, and the circulation portion with transportation uses such as highways and streets, mass transit,
and parking. Separate plans may be prepared for each of
the three components, and specialized plans may be prepared
for any single aspect of any of the components. Plans also
may be undertaken that do not fall into any of these three
categories. Increasingly, plans are directing attention
to the social and environmental implications and aspects
of physical development.
     The planning process includes the following steps:
(1) the establishment of community goals for desired future
growth and development; (2) data collection, research, and
studies in such areas as existing land uses, basic physical
features of the community, public facilities, transportation,
population characteristics, housing conditions, fiscal
capability and trends, economic and employment structure,
and perhaps environmental quality and social development
patterns; (3) the actual preparation of a plan or plans;
and (4) plan implementation.

PLANNING THEORY

     Planning theory holds that the various steps of the
planning process should follow an orderly and logical pattern. Community goals and objectives should be known before
plans are prepared. Extensive study of existing community
characteristics, problems, and opportunities should precede
planning for the future. Plans should be developed before
land uses are decided upon.
     Planning theory holds that certain designated govern-
mental powers should be used to carry out plans. These
powers include zoning and subdivision regulations and key
land-use controls that stipulate such things as land uses
permitted by law, layout patterns, public improvements to

be provided in new subdivisions, minimum lot sizes, and
maximum population densities. Other governmental powers
that can be used to implement plans include the official
map, which sets aside land for future public use; urban
renewal, which provides for the reuse of land; and code enforcement, which covers building construction, occupancy,
and maintenance matters. Other public powers, especially
those concerning highways and sewers, influence community
development, and, according to planning theory, these
powers should be exercised in a way that is consistent with
community planning.

A plan may specify the particular governmental powers
that will be called upon for its implementation and may
detail how land-use controls are to be used. Land-use controls like zoning and subdivision regulation are viewed in
planning theory as "tools" of planning; the primary mission
of these tools is to make the plan a reality.

Planning theory requires that land-use controls and
other governmental powers that impact on community development be understood and operate within the context of community planning. The argument is that if community development is to proceed along rational lines, standards are
needed, and planning provides the means for the consideration, adoption, and enforcement of these standards. The
theory is that with planning and plans, community development will be consciously directed, the likely impact of decisions will be known in advance, mistakes will be avoided,
future needs for public and private facilities will be an-
ticipated and met as they arise, resources will be set
aside prior to the time they are needed, and a more pleasing,
satisfying, and livable environment will ensue. All agencies and parties involved in community development are, by
planning theory, supposed to work within a common frame and
to have their activities judged by common standards provided
by community planning.

THEORY OF PLANNING ADMINISTRATION

Three organizational patterns in planning can be cited:
planning as a responsibility of an independent planning
commission; planning as a staff aid to the chief executive;
and planning as a function of the legislative body.

Planning theory originally held that planning should
be the function of an independent or semi-independent planning commission. Such a commission was to be part of municipal government but insulated from the general political

processes in municipalities. This theory was reflected in the Standard City Planning Enabling Act, published in 1928 by the U.S. Department of Commerce, and in other model planning acts. These model acts formed the base of planning-enabling legislation in most states, and this legislation prescribed the organization and powers of planning in localities.[7]

Advocates of the independent planning commission approach argue that this arrangement keeps politics out of planning, minimizes the influence of partisanship on planning, attracts better and more qualified people to planning boards, and is the organizational pattern most consistent with the differing roles of planners and elected officials. It is suggested that the political roles of elected officials may conflict with the professional demands of planning--that, for example, politicians cannot be expected to master a subject as complex as planning, and that politicians have short-range perspectives while planning requires a long-range outlook. Independent planning commissions are headed by boards whose members have fixed appointments usually not coinciding with the terms of elected officials. Partisans of the independent planning commission assume that planning board members will be respected citizens in the community who will represent the public interest in planning. The independent planning commission is the rule in most American communities.

Some communities have adopted other organizational arrangements, and a number of professional planners and others favor placing planning under the chief executive or the legislative body. A chief executive might be a mayor or city manager in municipalities, or the county executive or manager in counties. Mayors and county executives are elected by the people, while city and county managers are appointed by local governing bodies. Both elected and appointed chief executives are considered by political scientists to be politically responsive. Legislative bodies in cities and counties are elected by popular vote. Legislative bodies normally have the final say, and chief executives have considerable influence over most land-use controls and certain other key programs that help shape community development patterns regardless of who exercises the planning power.

Opponents of the independent planning commission argue that planning is essentially a political activity that cannot and should not be separated from the political processes; that since plan implementation powers usually rest with elected officials and not with planners, planning should be

placed under elected officials; that since operating programs (public works, for example) are under agencies outside the planning commission, the planning function should
be put under legislators or chief executives whose responsibilities include operating programs; that planning staffs
and politically responsive officials should develop close
ties to advance the ends of planning, a relationship virtually precluded under present arrangements; and that the
independent planning commission has been notably unsuccessful in promoting effective planning.

PLANNING AND THE FEDERAL SYSTEM

Local Planning. The kind of planning treated in this study
is that conducted mostly by municipalities, counties, townships, and towns. This can be considered local planning.
Local planning is normally undertaken by planning commissions serving the area within the jurisdiction of a given
political subdivision. Local planning is performed legally
within the authority of state legislation (usually enabling
legislation) or within the stipulations of a home-rule
charter. Local planning may be assisted under federal and
state grant programs.

Metropolitan Planning. Planning is also conducted at the
metropolitan level, normally by a metropolitan planning
commission or by a metropolitan council of governments.
Metropolitan planning commissions have limited powers, and
they may be created by local governments under (1) state
enabling legislation, the typical method, (2) by specific
acts of the state legislature, (3) by interstate compact,
or (4) by joint-exercise-of-powers statutes.[8] Metropolitan
planning commissions and metropolitan councils of governments may receive federal and state financial assistance.
The latter are distinguished from planning commissions
chiefly in their constituency base, being composed of
elected local government officials, whereas planning commissions are composed of a variety of interests, including
citizens (well-represented), appointed officials, and
elected officials.[9] Metropolitan planning is done for the
metropolitan area as a whole, which may include the jurisdiction of several municipalities, counties, and other local
governments. In 1967 the nation's 227 metropolitan areas
contained nearly 21,000 local governments, including municipalities, counties, townships, special districts, and school
districts--an average of slightly over 90 governments per

metropolitan area.[10] Metropolitan planning organizations
are rarely part of a general-purpose government unless they
are part of a county government and the county and metropolitan area boundaries coincide. Only five metropolitan areas
of the nation contain metropolitanwide municipal-type governments.

State Planning. States now undertake planning programs.
All states have designated a unit of state government to
handle general planning, and this agency includes the governor's office (20 states), a department of commerce or
economic development, a department of administration or
finance, an independent planning department, a department
of community affairs, or some other organization.[11] Statewide planning is still in its infancy, although recent
federal legislative and administrative actions promise to
strengthen it. A national land-use policy, currently under
consideration in Congress, could encourage stronger state
planning.

Regional Planning. Regional planning can be found in some
parts of the United States. A region may cover more than
a single state and may include a number of metropolitan
areas. Regionwide planning is presently most noticeably
being conducted by the various regional development commissions formed in the 1960s. These agencies include the Ap-
palachian Regional Development Commission (created under
federal law in 1965), and the Ozarks, New England, Upper
Great Lakes, Four Corners, and Coastal Plains Regional
Commissions (all created in accordance with the provisions
of the Public Works and Economic Development Act of 1965).

Rural Planning. Rural planning has only recently gotten under
way in America, and it lags considerably behind urban planning. Rural planning has concentrated on economic development. Unlike the situation in urban areas, no single organizational form characterizes the rural planning process.[12]
Among the most visible rural planning agencies are the economic development districts (EDDs); others include the rural
areas development committees (RADs) and soil and water conservation districts. Some states have been active in creating general planning districts for their rural areas.

National Planning. The national government has been prominently involved in promoting planning in urban communities
and other areas. Now urban planning assistance can be made
available to cities of any size (until recently it was lim-

ited to cities under 50,000), counties, and other local general-purpose governments; metropolitan and regional planning agencies; councils of governments; states; and rural agencies. The national government has also advanced the cause of community planning through its urban renewal assistance program. The federal government undertakes planning directly only in particular functional areas (such as recreation and airports), and this may be done on the basis of inputs provided by local and state governments. General planning is largely a subnational responsibility in the American federal system.

PARTICIPANTS IN THE PLANNING PROCESS

This study concentrates primarily on local planning and on the various forces that impact on the local planning process. Participants in the local planning process include representatives from other levels in the federal system, and these representatives may help shape the direction of community planning.

The planning process covers all decisions made in the preparation, adoption, and implementation of plans. Broadly, it includes not only planning decisions per se but zoning, subdivision regulation, and other key community development decisions that theoretically and sometimes actually fall within the scope of planning. A zoning decision, in other words, is considered part of the planning process whether or not a community has a planning commission or a published or adopted master plan. A decision can be part of the planning process even if no planning program, or no active one, exists. A zoning decision in a community that has a planning commission and an adopted plan is clearly a planning matter and qualifies as part of the planning process.

The participants in the planning process are as follows.

The Planning Board

The planning board stands at the pinnacle of the planning bureaucracy. It heads the independent planning commission. The planning board normally will have administrative authority over a planning staff. Of some 18,000 local governments that might be expected to have planning, about 10,700, or nearly 60 percent, have planning boards. Almost

90 percent of the cities with 5,000 or more population have planning boards. Planning boards contain an average of seven to eight members, and larger cities (50,000 or more population) have somewhat bigger boards.[13]

Planning boards are composed chiefly of citizen members, commonly appointed by local governing bodies or chief executives. Some boards have ex officio members, and these may include representatives of important local bureaucracies (such as public works). The planning board normally will have the power to adopt and revise master plans, and it will supervise the planning staff, which actually prepares the plans. The planning board has advisory power over basic zoning decisions (rezonings), although a special majority of the governing body (generally two-thirds or three-quarters) may be required to override planning boards' zoning recommendations. The planning board likely will have the final voice in the administration of subdivision regulations, may review site plans for proposed commercial or mixed commercial-residential developments, and may prepare and maintain the official map. The planning board may recommend amendments to the zoning ordinance text and may have advisory authority over local capital budget proposals.

The Planning Staff

The planning staff normally serves in a planning commission under the direction of the planning board. Some planning staffs operate directly under a chief executive, and some legislative bodies have their own internal planning staffs. The planning staff carries out duties as assigned, and it may constitute an independent political force in and of itself. The planning staff usually will be headed by a director, and staff responsibilities will be divided among different divisions or sections that report to the director.

Increasingly, planning staffs are becoming professional; they frequently include members with advanced degrees in planning and with membership in the American Institute of Planners (AIP), the organization of professional planners. Planning staffs may include persons trained in other fields --such as engineering, architecture, geography, or public administration--as well as in city planning.

The Chief Executive

The chief executive of the local government may have administrative authority over the planning staff, and he may appoint members of the planning board as well as the director of planning. The chief executive likely will attempt to serve key community interests in planning, and elected executives are particularly sensitive to the views of citizens associations. Although the chief executive usually does not make the basic decisions in planning, he coordinates the local agencies whose programs impact on the planning process, and, by virtue of his legal powers and his political resources, he may influence planning decisions made by the planning board, the planning staff, and the local governing body.

The Governing Body

The governing body plays an important part in the planning process--even when the planning function is administered by an independent planning commission. The governing body may appoint the planning board and may adopt plans. Governing boards, being elected bodies, are vulnerable especially to citizens association influence, particularly in smaller communities and when elected on a ward or district basis.

In most communities the governing body makes the final zoning decisions, including those concerning the text and map of the zoning ordinance. The text is the written provisions of the ordinance, and the map depicts the sections of the text that govern land use on each lot regulated by the ordinance. A change in the map is called a rezoning, and proposed rezonings typically take up most of the time a community governing body spends on planning matters. Other planning-related decisions may be made by the governing body.

The Courts

Several types of decision in the planning process may end up in the hands of the courts. For instance, zoning decisions of the governing body and subdivision decisions of the planning board may be taken to the state judiciary. The judiciary is, of course, bound by strict legal procedures and limited to cases brought to it; but courts may make determinations that affect given land uses and that have broad implications for future decisions in the planning process.

Citizens Associations

Citizens associations are organized on a neighborhood basis, and they commonly wield considerable power over planning and zoning decisions that affect particular neighborhoods. Citizens associations concentrate most attention on zoning decisions, and they usually seek rulings that preserve the status quo. Citizens groups support strong controls and restrictions on land development.

Developers

Developers and other real estate forces are key activists in the planning process. Included in this category are land developers, home builders, large landowners, and investors in private land and improvements. Real estate groups generally favor planning and zoning decisions that promote community growth and expansion. Developers are concerned with subdivision control decisions, and they work for public decisions that facilitate the development process. They frequently are organized into interest groups, known as builders associations, perhaps on a single jurisdiction (city, county), submetropolitan, or metropolitan-wide basis; realtors are organized separately into local boards of realtors.

State Roads Agencies

The most important highway agency in the federal system is the state roads department. State roads departments are responsible for the construction and maintenance of interstate and state highways; they receive assistance from the federal government for construction purposes. Cities, counties, and townships may have authority over local streets and highways.

State highway departments may exercise significant influence over community development, as highways tend to shape urban development patterns. State roads agencies do not have to adhere to community plans or zoning in making highway location decisions. As a result of the Federal-Aid Highway Act of 1962, all metropolitan areas now have a transportation planning process, in which state highway departments and local governments are to work cooperatively in planning highway projects. The transportation planning process may lead to a coordination of local planning and state highway programming.

Sewer and Water Districts

Sewer and water lines can influence development patterns. Decisions to extend sewer lines into undeveloped areas are particularly important in this respect. In the major metropolitan areas, the sewage disposal function is commonly assigned to special sewerage districts (the Metropolitan St. Louis Sewer District is an example). Water supply is frequently a function of special districts as well (there are over 2,000 urban water supply districts in the country).* Special districts with sewer and water responsibilities may have independent authority to locate sewer and water lines, and this authority may or may not be subject to advisory recommendations of the local planning commission or to the power of general-purpose local government (municipalities, counties).[14]

The General Business Community

General business interests participate in planning somewhat independently of the real estate community. In the larger metropolitan areas, developers are organized separately from the general business community; the former, as noted, work through builders associations (Minneapolis Home Builders Association, for example), while the general business community is organized into chambers of commerce or boards of trade.

In the planning process, the general business groups may support or oppose developers. The two do not necessarily have the same views on planning and zoning. General business groups, for example, may oppose rezonings that generate competition for existing businesses. The two are more likely to agree on broad planning principles and concepts than on specific rezoning proposals.

Boards of Adjustment

Most communities have a board of adjustment, a board of appeals, or a board of zoning appeals to consider granting special exceptions and variances to the zoning ordinance. Special exceptions, sometimes called special permits, con-

---

*Major sewer districts are now organized nationally into the Association of Metropolitan Sewerage Agencies.

cern uses not typical of a particular zoning category but
permitted by the zoning ordinance under certain conditions
(the location of a medical clinic in a residential zone
may be an example). Variances concern uses not consistent
with stipulations in the zoning ordinance but permitted if
compliance with the ordinance stipulations would involve
"unnecessary hardship" or "practical difficulty" (because
of unusual terrain conditions, for example). Boards of adjustment may grant or deny special exceptions and variances
and may have other authority as well.

Decisions made by boards of adjustment are not considered major ones by normal planning and zoning standards,
although it is possible that these decisions could have
marked effects in a single neighborhood. In some cases,
special exceptions are hotly contested. But basic zoning
decisions are not made by boards of adjustment; they are
made by the local governing body.

Education, Codes, Transit, Housing,
Renewal, and Airport Agencies

School districts, building and housing codes agencies,
urban mass transit authorities, public housing districts
and community development departments, urban renewal authorities, and airport agencies, all usually local government units, are concerned with decisions made in the planning process and may be affected by these decisions. These
agencies have programs that impact on community development.

Local school operations are significantly affected by
planning and zoning decisions, and school agencies may participate in these decisions. It is basic land-use decisions
that determine the number of children in the public schools
and the amount of available property taxes, a common source
of school financing. School location decisions and other
school agency determinations can affect community development patterns and may in turn be influenced by planning
policy.

Building and housing code agency decisions on building
and housing construction, maintenance, and occupancy can
affect environmental quality, housing conditions, and the
housing supply. Urban rail transit authority decisions on
the location of new transit lines, for example, can alter
community development patterns and affect planning and
zoning.

Decisions by public housing authorities and community
development departments can affect the housing quality and

housing supply for low- and moderate-income families, and urban renewal authority decisions can importantly mold land-use and reuse patterns in inner city areas. Airport bureaucracy decisions can influence urban development.

The education function in the community usually is handled by a special school district (nearly 22,000 of the 23,390 public school systems of the nation are run by special school governments), urban rail transit almost universally by a special district government (the Southeastern Pennsylvania Transportation Authority, SEPTA, in Philadelphia, is an example), public housing mostly by special districts, urban renewal not infrequently by special districts (there are over 2,000 housing and renewal authorities in the country), and airports often by special districts (Port of New York Authority, for example). The rail transit, public housing, urban renewal, and airport functions, when under special districts, normally are administered by governments called authorities.

Local planning agencies and key officials of general-purpose governments may play only a limited role in the decision-making processes of special districts,[15] and this may make coordinated community development and planning difficult. Regardless of how these local functions are administered (by special districts or by general-purpose governments), there is no assurance that they will be coordinated through a central planning process.[16]

Federal Agencies

The Department of Housing and Urban Development (HUD), a cabinet-level federal agency, has a noticeable effect on the community planning process. The influence of this agency in the community may be transmitted through its urban planning assistance (grant) program; through its workable program for community development, which covers community planning, codes, zoning, subdivision regulations, housing relocation, and other matters; through the private housing loan-underwriting activities of FHA, which may serve to mold community ordinances dealing with private housing; through its public housing program, which affects the operations of local housing authorities; through its urban renewal assistance program, which affects local renewal authorities; through its water, sewer, and neighborhood facilities grant program; through its model cities grant program; and through its open space grant program. In providing grants and other aid to localities, HUD sets standards for recipient agency operations and otherwise helps shape community development and planning decisions.

Other federal agencies that have an influence on community development and on the local planning process include the Department of Transportation (DOT), the Environmental Protection Agency (EPA), the Office of Economic Opportunity (OEO), and the Department of Agriculture (USDA). DOT, for example, provides grants to states and localities for highways, urban mass transit, and airport development. EPA advances money to special districts and other local governments to build sewage treatment facilities. OEO funds community action agencies (concerned mainly with social development), and USDA assists local and state agencies undertaking watershed projects. These departments have other programs that impact on community development and influence planning activities in the locality.

The federal government recently has taken significant action to stimulate the central coordination of federal and federally assisted projects at the state and local level. In accordance with federal law and administrative regulation, certain proposed federal activities are to be reviewed by central metropolitan, regional, and state clearinghouses. These clearinghouses may be planning agencies, councils of governments, economic development districts, or other organizations. Metropolitan clearinghouses are recognized by the federal government's Office of Management and Budget, and state and regional clearinghouses by the governor or state law. Metropolitan clearinghouses serve the metropolitan area as a whole, regional clearinghouses serve rural areas, and state clearinghouses serve the state as a whole. The clearinghouses are to ascertain the consistency of proposed federal action with state and community plans, development, and programming. The clearinghouses do not have veto power, but they may make recommendations. It is too early to assess the effects of these clearinghouses.

State Agencies

In addition to the state highway department, state agencies that may affect community development and influence the local planning decision-making process include the state planning department, the state economic development department, the state natural resources department and other natural resources agencies (parks, forests, water resource development, fish and wildlife activities, soil and water conservation), the state pollution control agency (a number of states now administer air and water pollution control programs in a single environmental quality agency),[17] and the state health department (sewage disposal rulings). Additionally, state legislators, especially those from the local community in question, may shape community development decisions. State legislation may have a significant affect on community development.[18] Governors also may play a role in setting local development policy.

Political Parties

Political parties cannot be overlooked. Both of the major political parties have some voice in the community planning process, and purely local parties (not Republican or Democratic) may have an important influence over community planning and zoning decisions. In planning and zoning, it is the local parties that count. These include the local units of the Republican and Democratic parties, and local parties not affiliated with the Republicans or Democrats.

Parties in the United States are not directed from the top down.[19] This means that local Republicans and Democrats are free to take independent stands on community development matters. In middle- and upper-income communities, both parties tend to support the citizens association point of view on planning policy, although exceptions can be cited. The national parties may influence community development policy by taking stands on certain legislation --such as housing, highway, and mass transit measures.

Purely local parties (such as the Arlingtonians for a Better County in Virginia) often have a basic interest in community planning decisions and tend to be status quo-minded on planning and zoning policy. The base of these parties, in fact, may be built around opposition to zoning changes and the preservation of single-family residential development.[20]

This is not an exhaustive list of the agencies and interests that are concerned with, that impact upon, or that are affected by community planning and development decisions and processes. But the major participants have been cited. No attempt has been made to assess their relative influence or effects, which may vary somewhat by community.

PLANNING AS PUBLIC POLICY

Academic interest in public policy has widened considerably in the past several years. Public policy analysis is being conducted in an ever-expanding number of areas,
and much comparative policy analysis has been undertaken
in the American state politics field.[21] Still, systematic
public policy analysis is a relatively new emphasis in the
social sciences. A growing body of literature in political
science is directed toward an explanation of the basic di-
mensions of public policy analysis and the basic elements
of the public policy processes.[22]

Public policy refers essentially to the major actions,
decisions, and statements of government and public officials.
The most visible source of public policy is legislation or
ordinances, but public policy also may be reflected in administrative regulations, judicial decisions, pronounce-
ments of key public officials, or other actions of government.

Public policy can be dissected further. We can consider public policy in terms of its goals. For instance,
in a 1968 enactment Congress set a housing production goal
of 26 million units over a ten-year period. We can consider policy in terms of its substantive content. Public
policy can cover, for example, transportation, education,
or pollution control matters. We also can view policy in
terms of the satisfactions it produces. Policies can produce "material" satisfactions--such as subsidies or power--
or they can produce "symbolic" satisfactions, moral and
psychological ones. Additionally, policies can be studied
from the standpoint of the level of government that makes
them (whether it be the national, state, or local level)
or from the standpoint of the government bureaucracy that
administers them (for example, a transportation department
administers transportation policy, a school board administers education policy).

Planning constitutes a policy area. Interpreted narrowly, planning policy refers to governmental actions directly connected to the master plan, including the preparation, consideration, adoption, and use of this plan. Interpreted broadly, planning policy refers to governmental
actions surrounding the master plan process and to governmental actions in the land-use control area, including zoning and subdivision regulation.

We also may talk about zoning policy. According to
the broader definition of planning policy, zoning policy
would be just one illustration of planning policy.   In
fact, it may be the most important one.   In communities
that do not have planning but do zone land, it is essential
to use the broader definition--in which case zoning policy
becomes planning policy.   In communities that have both
planning and zoning powers, and are not in reality doing
any planning but are zoning land, zoning policy becomes
planning policy.   Finally, in communities that are actively
undertaking planning programs, zoning may serve to shape
planning--in which case zoning policy again becomes planning policy.   This last case is not unusual, as we explain
later.

Planning policy should not be confused with "good" or
"positive" policy.   Some argue that planning based on private market principles is no policy at all.   But planning
can be based on any conception of community development,
no matter what the conception, who supports it, or what
its effects are.   Public policy that calls for private
market determination of land use (which may be reflected
in the refusal of a community to adopt a plan) qualifies
as planning policy, as does public policy that calls for
governmental control of land use.   (The authors, incidentally, support the concept of government control of land
use).

Similarly, policy in the planning area that is based
on the interests of functional bureaucracies--such as highway or sewer agencies--can be considered planning policy.
Some see this as no policy.   The authors, of course, support a more broadly based policy.

Planning policy differs from most other policy areas
in important respects.   For instance, planning policy encompasses activities that fall within other policy areas--
for example, it covers highways, and highways fall within
the transportation policy area.   In addition, the planning
policy area contains no basic operating programs; planners
do not construct highways, build subways, or operate schools.
Land-use controls are the most important set of powers in
the planning policy area--that is, if we interpret planning
policy in the broader sense.

Also, planning policy, unlike many other policies,
cannot be measured in terms of expenditure.   Many analyses
of public policy are based on the assumption that policy
can be effectively measured by studying spending patterns.
Analyses of highway, education, and welfare policies, for
example, have been undertaken by comparing state and local

22

governments' expenditures in these areas.[23] Different levels of expenditures (measured on a per capita basis) provide some indication of the nature and direction of public policy and permit the linking of varying expenditure patterns with such matters as turnout at the polls, the character of the political party system, the nature of organizational arrangements, and the stage of economic development. If conducted over a period of time, such studies allow the delineation of policy shifts as reflected in changing expenditure patterns.

PLANNING AND POLITICS

Planning is a distinctly political activity. Planning policy is made by human beings operating in a practical environment. Makers of planning policy have varying conceptions of the public interest and are subject to a wide variety of governmental and political pressures. Different groups in the planning process view the ends and means of planning differently. Unanimity does not exist and cannot be expected. A certain degree of conflict is healthy, and in a democracy it will be found whether it is healthy or not. It is this conflict that makes for politics.

It is easier to arrive at a consensus over the generalities of planning than it is to reach agreement about specifics. For example, all participants in the planning process believe that the public interest should prevail over private interest and that good planning is better than its opposite. Yet there is disagreement over precisely what that public interest is and how good planning specifically is to be achieved. There is commonly much disagreement over particular zoning decisions and highway locations --even where there has been agreement on a plan calling for such decisions or highway locations. This reflects the nature of the American political process, and planning decision-making is no exception.

Increasingly, the planning literature has stressed the political character of planning.[24] This represents a decided shift from the earlier posture of the professional planning community. This shift, it seems, has been both inevitable and healthy. It reflects a recognition of the reality facing planning all across the nation, and it sets the stage for a more active and aggressive planning agency. Planners can help shape the community political process, and there is no reason why they should not seek to do so.

There is another dimension to the discussion of planning politics. Some contend that planning decisions should be made on the basis of expert views and professional values. This assumes that there are a set of impartial standards that can readily form the base for practical planning decisions. However true this may be (and this study assumes it is), these standards can be registered in planning decision-making only through the political process. They will be registered only to the extent that the political process permits. There is no way of avoiding this so long as basic planning decisions are made by governments. We must, in the final analysis, deal with this reality.

This brings up another point. Many participants in the planning process are not professional planners. This would include most governing body members, most planning board members, most chief executives, most citizens association leaders, most developers, and most of the others concerned with planning decision-making. This has many implications, but it may mean that many of the participants will not be able to work satisfactorily with professionally esoteric analyses of planning matters. This may lead to decisions being made on the basis of studies and information that are not fully understood by the decision-makers, and it may lead to a rejection of useful but complex inputs.

EFFECTS OF PLANNING POLICY

Planning policy is generally made in the community and subject to local and other pressures. But its effects are felt both in the community and beyond. The effects are of a physical, social, economic, and political nature. They may have implications for the metropolitan area as a whole, states, regions, the nation at large, and may even be registered abroad.

Local planning, insofar as it can serve to segregate the population along economic or racial lines, may well affect the way other nations view us. It can effect the way public policy is made at other levels in the political system, especially by shaping patterns of representation in state legislatures and Congress. And this could have consequences for the substance of public policy in a variety of functional areas, including education, health care, civil rights, crime control, transportation, pollution control, and foreign policy. Different political views on these topics are often traced to an economic base;[25] therefore, the effects of planning and land-use policy may be wide indeed.

NOTES

1. F. Stuart Chapin, Jr., Urban Land Use Planning (Urbana: University of Illinois Press, 1965). This work is often used in introductory city planning courses.

2. Donald H. Webster, Urban Planning and Municipal Public Policy (New York: Harper & Row, 1958).

3. T. J. Kent, Jr., The Urban General Plan (San Francisco: Chandler Publishing Co., 1964).

4. Alan Altshuler, The City Planning Process: A Political Analysis (Ithaca, N.Y.: Cornell University Press, 1965).

5. See, for example, Francine F. Rabinovitz, City Politics and Planning (New York: Atherton Press, 1969). Altshuler, cited above, is also a political scientist. Edward C. Banfield, a prominent political scientist, has had a long-standing interest in planning.

6. See Bernard J. Frieden and Robert Morris, eds., Urban Planning and Social Policy (New York: Basic Books, 1968). Several contributors to this volume are sociologists, including Herbert J. Gans, Lee Rainwater, and Robert A. Dentler.

7. For a thorough discussion of alternative administrative arrangements in planning, see David C. Ranney, Planning and Politics in the Metropolis (Columbus, Ohio: Charles E. Merrill, 1969), pp. 49-60.

8. National Survey of Metropolitan Planning, U.S. Housing and Home Finance Agency (Washington, D.C.: Government Printing Office, 1963), p. 4.

9. 1964 National Survey of Metropolitan Planning, U.S. Housing and Home Finance Agency (Washington, D.C.: Government Printing Office, 1965), p. 5.

10. Census of Governments 1967, Vol. 1, Governmental Organization, U.S. Bureau of the Census (Washington, D.C.: Government Printing Office, 1968), p. 10.

11. Robert M. Cornett, "Planning, Housing and Development," in Robert H. Weber, ed., The Book of the States 1970-1971 (Lexington, Ky.: Council of State Governments, 1970), p. 441.

12. James L. Sundquist, Making Federalism Work (Washington, D.C.: The Brookings Institution, 1969), especially chaps. 4 and 5.

13. Allen D. Manvel, Local Land and Building Regulation, National Commission on Urban Problems, Research Report No. 6 (Washington, D.C.: Government Printing Office, 1968), pp. 4, 9, 23.

14. Building the American City, National Commission on Urban Problems (Washington, D.C.: Government Printing Office, 1968), p. 232.

15. For a critical treatment of special districts, see The Problem of Special Districts in American Government, Advisory Commission on Intergovernmental Relations (Washington, D.C.: Government Printing Office, 1964).

16. See, for instance, Scott Greer, Urban Renewal and American Cities (Indianapolis: Bobbs-Merrill, 1965), pp. 76-78.

17. Elizabeth H. Haskell, Victoria Price, et al., Managing the Environment: Nine States Look for New Answers (Washington, D.C.: Woodrow Wilson International Center for Scholars, 1971).

18. William H. Whyte, The Last Landscape (Garden City, N.Y.: Doubleday, 1968).

19. See V. O. Key, Jr., Politics, Parties and Pressure Groups, 5th ed. (New York: Thomas Y. Crowell, 1964); and Clinton Rossiter, Parties and Politics in America (Ithaca, N.Y.: Cornell University Press, 1960).

20. Franklin O. Felt, "A Study of Nonpartisan Political Organization: The Arlingtonians for a Better County (ABC)" (Ph.D. thesis, Michigan State University, 1961).

21. See, for instance, Ira Sharkansky, Spending in the American States (Chicago: Rand McNally, 1968); Wayne L. Francis, Legislative Issues in the Fifty States (Chicago: Rand McNally, 1967); and Thomas R. Dye, Politics, Economics, and the Public: Policy Outcomes in the American States (Chicago: Rand McNally, 1966).

22. The recent public policy literature includes Charles O. Jones, An Introduction to the Study of Public Policy (Belmont, Calif.: Wadsworth Publishing Co., 1970); Austin Ranney, ed., Political Science and Public Policy (Chicago: Markham Publishing Co., 1968); Charles E. Lindblom, The Policy-Making Process (Englewood Cliffs, N.J.: Prentice-Hall, 1968); Randall B. Ripley, ed., Public Policies and Their Politics (New York: W. W. Norton, 1966); and Allan P. Sindler, ed., American Political Institutions and Public Policy (Boston: Little, Brown, 1969).

23. One of the first collections of comparative state policy studies in these issue areas was Herbert Jacob and Kenneth N. Vines, eds., Politics in the American States: A Comparative Analysis (Boston: Little, Brown, 1965). Comparative local government policy studies can be found in James Q. Wilson, ed., City Politics and Public Policy (New York: John Wiley, 1968).

24. See, for instance, Thad L. Beyle and George T. Lathrop, eds., Planning and Politics (New York: Odyssey Press, 1970).

25. Many studies have demonstrated this. These include V. O. Key, Jr., Public Opinion and American Democracy (New York: Alfred A. Knopf, 1961); Angus Campbell, et al., The American Voter (New York: John Wiley, 1960); and (more recently) Lloyd A. Free and Hadley Cantril, The Political Beliefs of Americans: A Study of Public Opinion (New York: Simon and Schuster, 1968). Landmark voting studies that show the economic roots to political beliefs include Paul F. Lazarsfeld, Bernard Berelson, and Hazel Gaudet, The People's Choice (New York: Columbia University Press, 1948); and Angus Campbell, Gerald Gurin, and Warren E. Miller, The Voter Decides (Evanston, Ill.: Row, Peterson, 1954).

CHAPTER

2

PLANNING—
THE LOST ART

Lewis Mumford tells us that planning is not new, that
planning has been going on for centuries, in different
forms and with varying degrees of success.[1] What has happened in the past may be open to some speculation, but
what is happening in the United States here and now is not.
If we have planning, it is not obvious to the casual ob-
server, if indeed it is to anyone. The nation's colleges
and universities typically give courses in urban planning
and design, and a number offer advanced degrees in the
field, up to and including the doctor of philosophy. The
most common degree program in planning, the master's degree
in city planning (or urban planning or urban and regional
planning) includes a variety of individual courses covering
an ever-increasing number of subjects treating different
aspects of this currently highly popular concentration.

As if this were not enough, books on city planning and
the urban environment often tell us of the need for comprehensive planning and the advantages of undertaking planning
programs. Young people, students, and others are deluged
with facts and figures about urban planning, with techniques of proper planning, with principles of good land
use, and with sundry data on urban development--all of
which familiarize them with the abstractions in the planning
field but which do not explain the reality of American
planning politics and the practice of planning today. To
put it simply, we do not have planning--not in its ideal
form, not in its less than ideal form; in short, not at
all. What passes for planning is a sham--it is not planning at all, and it is wrong to pass it off to the untutored
as planning of any kind.

In planning, an enormous gap exists between the ideal
and the real, and this gap keeps people from acquiring the

knowledge they need to make judgments and to effect change on the urban scene. Why does this gap exist? Well, in part because what is <u>found</u> in American communities is so often at variance with what is taught and written about them. It is not as though what is taught or written is designed deliberately to deceive (or to sell, though this motivates some), but it is true that much of what is said about planning in the classroom and in the literature is based on what students or readers want or expect, or is merely someone's conception of what should exist (but is not identified as such). Those not involved in planning and land-use politics, and often those who are involved in one way or another, have virtually no basis on which to determine the accuracy of the various statements made on the subject. It is only natural, then, that what has resulted is a combination of idealizations, abstractions, hucksterism, professionalism, and (even) facts.

THE FUTURE OF URBAN DEVELOPMENT

No matter what one reads or hears, one cannot be misled by one's own observation. Metropolitan America is in a mess, and the consequences of not doing something about this mess can be tragic. One need cite only a few of the numerous fields in which we have failed to achieve or even approach our objectives--housing, the environment, transportation, and sewer and water systems are illustrative. There is no evidence that matters are getting better; it even appears to us that we may be moving backward in some respects. Nevertheless, positive change is not only quite possible but also it is bound to be effected in time.

Edward C. Banfield pictures urban America in terms of certain "imperatives"--imperatives that constrain and dictate basic metropolitan growth and development patterns. According to Banfield, little or nothing can be done by government to alter these imperatives or the essential "logic of metropolitan growth," and government must work within the logic of the metropolitan growth processes.[2] Despite the limits of public policy in dealing with metropolitan development and with the basic forces controlling this development, there are certain tools, mechanisms, ideas, and concepts that man can draw upon to reverse certain trends and to modify directions in urban development, including both physical and social development.

Do we have to accept urban sprawl as a permanent feature of the metropolitan environment? Are we forced to live with transportation networks that do not move people where (or when) they want to go? Must we suffer the continuing blight of ghettos--ghettos hemmed in and perpetuated by governmental and social pressures? Must we resign ourselves to residential economic segregation throughout the metropolitan regions? Or can we do something about these conditions?

The authors assume that sound judgments about planning and the many other issues in urban development can be made only by knowing and understanding the facts. It is for this reason that the practice of planning is emphasized. Theorizing is not excluded; nor is philosophy. But, to a certain extent, the purpose of this work is to instruct, and to do so by presenting to the reader material that more or less dictates its own direction. Experience is a good teacher, and in planning and urban development there has been abundant experience to draw on. Rational inquiry into any field likely will lead to certain conclusions that will form the basis of recommendations for change. It is in this spirit that the reader should explore the facts, ideas, and conclusions presented in this study and relate them to his own community. It is hoped that they may serve to help set directions of desirable urban development policy.

We have seen planning and urban development in most of its various stages and in its different geographical, social, economic, and political settings, and in this study we have to identify studies and source materials in urban planning, political science, sociology, urbanology, and other fields that will help explain what is at this moment taking place in the fields of planning and metropolitan development. Theory is important, and theory keyed to practical reality is one crucial type of theory that can take us out of the posture of drift and decay that are so characteristic of planning and urban development today. A frank assessment of our situation suggests that our basic existing institutions are capable of producing important change--and a new era in urban development. Our task is to achieve a realistic understanding of these institutions and their capabilities.

Important features of a nation's political, economic, and social systems serve to shape all forces impacting upon these systems. Solutions in planning and urban development founded on unworkable abstractions are apt to divert us from our central concern and to consume an unwarranted amount of time and energy. Particularly liable to such snares are planning and development solutions that purportedly work in certain environments and countries and that are proposed for use elsewhere. Such solutions may not be applicable in nations that have political, economic, and social systems that contrast sharply with those in the country or environment where such approaches are used.

It is not uncommon for students of planning and urban development to propose adoption of courses of action in the United States that are used in other nations. Such proposals may be made in the most serious and sincere of manners, and sometimes they are backed by policy makers even though no one knows whether they will work or whether they are applicable to the American setting.[3] All of which reminds us of what Daniel P. Moynihan said in his book on community action projects: "Enough snake oil has been sold in this Republic to warrant the expectation that public officials will begin reading labels."[4]

COMPREHENSIVE PLANNING

Planning is not new. In the Western world, the history of urban planning alone can be traced to the ancient period, and considerable evidence of planning can be cited at the town level in the Middle Ages and since. Planning can, of course, be undertaken in a variety of settings and by different organizations; it is found to some extent in virtually every social institution in existence. We are here concerned specifically with urban planning. The more recent term "comprehensive planning" also can be used to describe the process that concerns us--a process, broadly speaking, that provides for the establishment of goals in community development and land use and for the various programs and efforts designed to achieve these goals. In the past, planning of this variety concentrated on physical development. In recent years the scope of planning has been broadened, and now planners direct attention to social phenomena and related factors. But urban planning activity always has had an effect on the social features of the community and there always has been a tie between the physical (including, generally, the economic) and the social aspects of community development--a tie that perhaps is being recognized and emphasized now. Also, the current emphasis on social development in planning has certain value overtones, as it represents an attempt on the part of the more progressive forces in the planning community to place the planning process on the side of social change.

31

THE LOCAL NATURE OF PLANNING

The important planning in America, in both the administrative and policy senses, nearly always is conducted at the local level. The country has no nationwide comprehensive plan, no national action program to set directions for future urban development; it has been only in the last few years that more than a handful of states have done any work in comprehensive planning.

Urban planning is a municipal, county, township, or town responsibility. Nearly all cities in the metropolitan areas of the nation, including central cities and suburban municipalities, have a planning board, and the planning board typically sits at the top of the local planning administrative structures (see Chapter 1). Further, most American cities of any size have a published master plan, the initial product of the planning process. Incidentally, this tells us little or nothing about whether the communities with planning boards and master plans are taking any action that is affecting community development--it only tells us that these boards and plans exist. It also tells us nothing about whether the planning boards have adopted the plans drawn up by their own staffs, or whether community governing bodies that have plan implementation powers have ever adopted these plans, or have even read them. In fact, more communities appear to be "doing" planning than doing anything about it.

The typical planning agency covers the jurisdiction of a single locality--that is, a single political subdivision--and each metropolitan area is likely to contain literally dozens of political subdivisions that have their own planning commissions and planning powers. The planning operation is an arm of local government.

As noted in the Introduction, planning that is conducted across local jurisdiction lines, sometimes including the entire metropolitan area, is found throughout the United States, but planning agencies functioning at this level commonly have only the most limited authority. The real power over planning, to the extent that such power exists at all, resides in the community. The land-use controls that can be used to carry out plans are almost exclusively among the responsibilities of local governments, not metropolitan or interjurisdictional bodies.

That planning has been a local matter in this country can be attributed to tradition more than anything else, and it is interesting to observe in this regard that although the United States has backed UN policy urging national plan-

ning in underdeveloped countries the United States to this
day has no national planning program itself.

There are a number of good arguments for having planning done at the local level. These include the following:

1. The people closest to the problems can best solve
them.
2. Local control of planning assures the grass-roots
support that is vital to success.
3. Land-use controls are handled locally, and therefore planning should be also.
4. Other key community development decisions are made
locally, so it is natural that planning would be a local
matter.
5. Local control over planning best conforms to the
general nature of the distribution of powers in our federal
system.

It is not suggested that these arguments are good in
the sense that they always accord with the reality of the
situation. They are advanced here only because these are
points that are commonly made and because at least some of
them have theoretical validity. On the other hand, one
would be hard pressed to state categorically that any process or activity of government is purely local,[5] and this
applies to planning. A strong argument can be made that
planning is one of the least local of all governmental functions, in view of the fact that community development matters are not limited to a single jurisdiction as is planning, and that almost anything that is done in planning has
to have some implications for other jurisdictions, for the
metropolitan area as a whole, or for the region of which
the community is only a part. It may make more sense to
have program implementation than planning decision-making
powers in local governments.

Additionally, communities and their governments in
this country have been known to act in the most arbitrary
of ways. This action is not limited to the South. Such
action may well stem from the local character of government
power. As we have been told by our founding fathers, local
may also mean parochial; it may mean oppressive majoritar-
ianism, it may mean absence of diversity, and it may mean
bad public policy. In urging adoption of a strong national
government, James Madison said that a rage for "improper
and wicked" policies is more apt to pervade smaller than
larger areas, and that private interest-motivated factions
too often control public policy processes in restricted and

narrow republics.[6] Today, local rule in planning and land
use can and does frequently spell racial discrimination,
economic segregation, and social class division.

It is no doubt in the light of the undesirable effects
of local control of planning that some have put their political muscle behind proposals to shift planning determinations upward in the political system--particularly proposals to place planning in the hands of metropolitan authorities. Certainly, many of those who have backed metropolitan government (single government for the metropolitan
area as a whole) have been motivated at least in part by
the wish to see planning conducted on a broader basis than
it presently is. Metropolitan planning is a tempting idea,
and we support metropolitan government, but of a certain
type (see Chapter 6). With metropolitan government one is
more likely to get metropolitan planning--that is, meaningful planning. Metropolitan planning with metropolitan government is sensible; metropolitan planning without metropolitan government is like constructing a house without a
foundation, for no governmental structure would exist to
back up the planning.

But before going too far into the metropolitan government idea, it should be pointed out that the record of attempts to establish metropolitan government is dismal indeed. Only a few examples of metropolitan government can
be cited in the United States--Metropolitan Dade County
(Miami), Jacksonville, Nashville, Baton Rouge, and Indianapolis. In each case, a municipal type of government exists
for the metropolitan area as a whole, although local or
municipal governments also may be found within the metropolitan area (in the Miami area, 27 municipal governments
are an integral part of the metropolitan federation that
forms the governing system for Dade County). The fact is
that when the voters have been given a chance they nearly
always have turned down proposals for metropolitan government, and the prospects for metropolitan government in the
future do not appear particularly bright. Suburban voters
traditionally have been hostile to metropolitan government,
as have, generally, inner-city blacks. Suburban residents
rarely have been more favorably inclined to metropolitan
government than have city residents. As the black population and voice in central cities grow, perhaps cities will
be about as antagonistic to metropolitan government as
suburbs.[7]

Areawide planning appears to be effective in Metropolitan Dade County. Areawide planning in Dade County is
basically a responsibility of the Planning Advisory Board

and the county Planning Department (the board and department are separate). The Planning Advisory Board is appointed
by the governing body (Board of County Commissioners), and
the Planning Department is under the County Manager. The
Board of County Commissioners has approved by resolution
a "General Land Use Master Plan" for the area served by
the metropolitan government. The plan is designed to
guide land-use control decisions at both the metropolitan
and municipal levels. The metropolitan government has the
subdivision control power over the entire county, including
the area inside municipalities, and a countywide subdivision
control ordinance has been adopted by the metropolitan governing body. The metropolitan government has the zoning
authority for the areas outside incorporated municipalities,
while municipal governments zone land inside municipal
boundaries. About 800,000 of the metropolitan area's 1.3
million residents live within municipalities.

Metropolitan planning in Dade County is stronger than
it might have been because the metropolitan government has
the power to set minimum performance and service standards
for municipalities.* Failure of the municipality to comply
may result in the metropolitan government's taking over
the affected function or service. So far, the metropolitan
government has set minimum standards for only a few activities, including housing regulations and building codes.
The power to establish these standards--along with the
subdivision control authority--provides the metropolitan
government with important tools that help assure implementation of the areawide master plan. Still, it is not clear
that municipal zoning decisions are based on the areawide
master plan. Zoning might be another area in which metropolitanwide standards might be set by the central government at some point in the future.

In all of the other four metropolitan governments, areawide planning is under the metropolitan government, although
it is being conducted with varying degrees of success.
Even with a metropolitan government, planning still may be
done at the local level, as it is to some extent in Metropolitan Dade County (the City of Miami, for example). Presumably, such planning is more "local" and detailed in nature than the areawide variety.

_____

*This power is spelled out in "The Home Rule Amendment
and Charter," Metropolitan Dade County, Florida. The state
authorized adoption of this charter in 1956; it was adopted
in 1957 and amended in 1961, 1962 (twice), 1963, 1966, 1967,
and 1969.

Other means of curtailing the planning power of the locality have been generally unsuccessful. These include the creation of metropolitan councils of government and bolstering the position of existing metropolitanwide planning agencies. Scores of councils of governments exist, and metropolitan planning agencies are now located in all parts of the United States; but in both cases their planning duties and their impact on planning and land use in the community do not amount to much. With both councils of government and metropolitan planning commissions, we are faced with a situation in which a superstructure exists without a foundation. Metropolitan planning commissions typically represent citizens and not local government officials in the area. Councils of government, while composed of local elected officials, do not represent officials explicitly chosen to carry out metropolitanwide assignments. Neither has any significant political or administrative base.

Councils of government received a mighty boost with the enactment of certain federal legislation in 1965 and 1966; but these units, which represent local elected officials on a metropolitanwide basis, have not in the main developed strong planning programs that serve to tie the efforts of individual municipalities together in a unified fashion. Metropolitan planning commissions have been traditionally weak, and little has happened in the past several years to change their political position in the metropolitan area scheme of things. The basic planning and land-use power still resides in the locality. To what extent the new federal program review power will affect the political status of councils of government and metropolitan planning commissions cannot be determined at this time (see Chapter 1).

The local assignment of planning is bound to continue, at least for the time being, although such an assignment may not be ideal. The exercise of the planning authority at the local level raises serious questions, but it cannot be argued that the only real problem with planning is that it is locally administered, or that the planning process could be improved substantially solely by transferring the authority to a metropolitan government (even if more of these existed), or to the state or national governments. Put slightly differently, there are definitely a number of problems in planning as we know it today, but these problems cannot be solved merely by shifting planning responsibilities upward in the political system; nor is it accurate to say that these problems exist only because planning is conducted at the local level. Local control of planning is, it appears, something that we will have to live with; but even with a change in the level of assignment of this function, without other substantive changes planning would not necessarily have advanced beyond its present position.

In the following sections of this chapter, we turn to the substance of planning and to a critical analysis of planning in the American community. We shall discuss the planning process and areas of weakness and strength, and we shall advance ideas about how planning can be improved.

THE FAILURE OF COMPREHENSIVE
PLANNING

We do not really have planning. That is, in most communities throughout the United States, we do not have planning that has any meaning. It is true that we have examples of planning done by government, but it is rarely the kind of planning discussed in this chapter--urban, or comprehensive, planning. We do have special-function planning, planning that is done in particular policy or departmental areas, but this, of course, is not the same thing as comprehensive planning. For instance, highway departments plan-- perhaps not always in the way that we would wish, but they plan nevertheless. So do sewer districts, water agencies, urban renewal authorities, public works departments, and mass transit bureaucracies. The planning that is done by such special-function units is "meaningful"--that is, it is planning that has a good chance of being carried out, a good chance of becoming program reality. We shall return to this matter of functional planning shortly.

Probably the best evidence of the lack of planning today is found by observing the world around us--the typical metropolitan area. It is not necessary that the average American know anything about planning and the operations of planning agencies; all he has to do is look about him, and he recognizes that planning is not taking place.

There is one major exception to this assessment (aside from functional planning), and this is the planning that is done in a number of surburban areas inhabited by middle- and upper-income residents. In such areas, planning is still not conducted as it should be, but it is conducted; plans are prepared, goals set, and action consistent with the plan is taken. But in these areas, planning is often a formality to provide professional legitimacy to the exclusionary, antidevelopment, and anticommercial policies already reflected in zoning and subdivision practices. Planning in such cases frequently does not precede the formulation of land-use policies in zoning and subdivision control ordinances; planning follows the development of such policies. Nevertheless, this planning can have its independent effects. It is hard to accept this as planning, although it is normally so interpreted.

When we indicate that planning is not being done or not being done properly, when we point to urban areas characterized by congestion, overcrowding, sprawl, and disorder in land use, this is not meant to imply that there is some sort of conspiracy against planning, or against good planning. The conspiracy theory is popular in some circles, although the nature of the conspirators varies with the group making the allegations.

Most commonly, developers, builders, and the real estate community in general are the targets. It is held that these forces are attempting to undermine community planning, and for their own private, selfish, and profit-seeking ends. As the reasoning goes, if we can just stop these forces, perhaps run them out of the community, proper planning will be instituted and all will live happily ever after. In view of our private enterprise system, it is not clear who would then do the building.

It may surprise some people to learn that the real estate community often has similar thoughts about citizens associations. Developers question the motives of citizens association leaders, contending that the real concern of these leaders is not the betterment of the community but their own political advancement or popularity, that they are working out their frustrations as overeducated government or corporate clerks, or that their objectives are social, not substantive. The developer commonly views citizens associations as reactionary forces that strive to keep any new business and most residential development out of their neighborhoods. The real estate community typically rejects the citizens association perception of itself as a progressive element of the local political system, working for the advancement of the public interest. Both citizens associations and real estate groups are apt at times to attack public officials, complaining of corruption or a "sell-out" to private interests (that is, to real estate or citizens forces, respectively). Regardless of the political charges, developers and builders have a job to do in the community, an important one, and citizens associations have legitimate interests to protect.

No one in land-use politics is consciously and systematically seeking to sabotage community planning efforts. Few

actors in planning have as their sole or primary aim personal profit or political aggrandizement. At least the
participants in planning politics do not view themselves
in this light, and this is what counts. We shall not discuss every group that has something to say about community
planning (a full listing is found in Chapter 1), but the
comments apply to other interests as well (to planning
boards and professional planners, for example). No one
familiar with the main forces involved in planning can say
decisively that this or that interest is at the root of
the problem. In fact, a variety of groups and individuals
have important interests in planning, and they are all here
to stay. They all probably will continue to advance their
respective interests in planning and to have a say in the
planning decision-making process.

Although it is common to "explain away" the actions
of one's assumed adversary in planning as motivated by private interest, and although it is common for each group to
stand in judgment of its adversary's (or others') motives,
careful examination will reveal that most of the major
forces in planning politics consider themselves to be motivated by the public interest. That groups and individuals
differ on the specifics of what constitutes the public interest in planning simply suggests that different interests
have different conceptions of the public good. That someone or some force reaps political reward or financial gain
from planning decisions does not necessarily mean that this
was the primary or sole motivating factor. Most actors in
planning see themselves as working for the good of the community, perhaps along with personal gain, and the two do
not have to be incompatible.

THE CASE OF FUNCTIONAL PLANNING

Earlier in this chapter, it was indicated that planning is being successfully undertaken in particular functional areas; planning by specific government bureaucracies
with operating programs can be considered functional planning. The agencies that are doing functional planning have
much to do with shaping current development patterns in the
metropolitan area. Such agencies therefore have to share
the blame for present problems. The powers of these agencies have been used to carry out specialized plans, whether
or not these plans are consistent with what comprehensive
planning may dictate. Thus, no matter who dominates the
formal planning process in the community, no matter who
controls the comprehensive planning agency, it is entirely

possible that one or more of the bureaucracies with special-
function planning and operating programs would serve to
work against the development goals of this controlling interest. This adds another dimension to the general confusion surrounding community land-use politics.

There are reasons why specialized agencies have been
more successful in their planning efforts than comprehensive planning organizations. In many functional areas, for
example, there are accepted standards that serve as the
basis of planning for particular programs. In highway
planning, for instance, one can count traffic flows, conduct
origin and destination studies, and build models; with the
results of such analyses, one can plan new highways and
their locations. Standards that permit such study do not
exist in comprehensive planning, and this makes it harder
to "sell" and to gain real support for comprehensive planning in the community. Comprehensive planning is more
"general" and vague.

Further, in specific functional areas in which operating programs are found, the planning and implementation
powers are located in the same agency--the highway bureaucracy, for example, contains both the planners and builders
of roads (technically, the construction is done privately
but at public direction), and urban renewal authorities
exercise both planning and execution powers. In comprehensive planning, on the other hand, the planning agency has
no authority to carry out its plans--not in any clear and
definitive sense anyway.

Finally, the typical single-function bureaucracy with
operating powers often has important clients and constituents who provide the agency with political backing and
who serve to protect and advance the agency's interests in
a variety of ways. Roads agencies, for example, are supported by key highway building, automobile manufacturing,
rubber, oil, and trucking interests. At least in the early
years, urban renewal authorities were backed by powerful
downtown business interests. Comprehensive planning agencies rarely enjoy such a political support base.

THE RECENT HISTORY OF PLANNING
DECISION-MAKING

Certain political patterns have characterized the planning decision-making process over the years, and there are
patterns that are emerging at present. It has not been uncommon for the real estate community to take the political

lead in planning. Since the 1920s, when planning as we know it today first originated in this country, and particularly since the 1940s and 1950s, when planning became a visible and recognizable force in communities, up to the early 1960s, real estate forces appear to have been well represented on planning commissions.[8] Not realtors but builders and developers and those that work with them (architects, for example) are usually the key real estate forces concerned with planning decisions. Real estate interests are organized for political action in local government.

The fact that they are directly involved in activities affected by planning decisions early led real estate people to seek positions as spokesmen in public planning agencies. This involvement has been natural in view of the knowledge and expertise that real estate people had in planning and land-use matters. Of course, their economic stakes in development served as a key stimulating force. The real estate influence in planning was generally of a subtle and indirect character--outright power plays were rare. And such tactics are often the most effective.

Following World War II a new interest in planning became evident in numerous American communities, and this interest ultimately gained formal recognition through neighborhood improvement and citizens associations. This force was particularly active in newly developing city and suburban areas. In the 1950s, this new interest, whether organized formally or not, began to wield power over planning decisions, particularly in zoning. In some areas in the late 1950s, and in more areas in the 1960s, citizens groups managed to become the decisive influence over the planning decision-making process. By the early 1970s, community after community had fallen into the hands of such interests, and planning and land-use policy decisions were shaped to their desires. As power was being shifted from real estate to citizens groups in different parts of the country, there was considerable struggle and conflict in the planning process. The vestiges of this conflict remain in a number of communities. In some areas, there was a relatively long period in which the two basic interests were somewhat evenly balanced. Many key development decisions were made during this period, and the situation did not contribute to good planning and properly guided land development. The tendency was for each side to force its views when it had a temporary majority.

The results of community planning have not been any better when the process has been dominated by citizens as-

sociations than they were when it was influenced by real
estate interests or characterized by a conflict between
the two. Planning, in fact, may have retrogressed with
this new control pattern. The transfer of power to this
new group has, for instance, given us additional urban
sprawl, this time in the form of endless large-lot development and uninterrupted subdivisions of exclusively single-
family homes on individual lots. Wherever the new controlling force has seized power, it successfully has pressed
government to curtail the rate of commercial and industrial
growth, if not, indeed, to eliminate altogether the possibility of new business moving into the community. Citizens
associations are discussed in Chapter 5.

THE PLANNING PROCESS

The community plan may be called master plan, general
plan, comprehensive plan, or land-use plan. The terms can
be used interchangeably, although particular communities
may use one or another or may use more than one and apply
them to different plans. The land-use plan may have a more
specific meaning (private uses of land).

For larger local communities, the planning process is
often divided into two interdependent stages: planning
for the entire area within the jurisdiction of the locality
and planning for particular neighborhoods, districts, or
subareas within the locality. The planning done for the
entire area will be more general in scope than that done
for subareas; the plan covering the whole area may outline
in broad form desired future development patterns, while
the plan treating subareas may detail the proposed future
land use lot by lot or tract by tract. There may be some
overlap between the two levels.

In smaller communities there may be only a single
plan for the entire area, and this plan is likely to contain rather specific proposals for future uses. Even plans
developed in larger communities for the entire land area
of the jurisdiction may be, in fact, highly specific in
designating desired future land uses.

A master plan typically will contain both a map indi-
cating proposed future development and a text that explains
the rationale, principles, and policies behind the plan as
well as the steps needed to implement the plan. The plan
also may discuss the status of planning in the community
and name the official participants in the plan preparation,
adoption, and implementation processes. The master plan

may be reinforced with other plans (community facilities, for example), and in addition there may be a plan for the metropolitan area as a whole or for a portion of the metropolitan area extending beyond the locality's boundaries.

WHAT'S WRONG WITH MASTER PLANS?

Plans Contain Too Much Specificity

Ideally, plans should be general. It is clear that many plans, perhaps most of them, are not. Even master plans that cover larger communities are by no means uniformly general in content. Subarea plans are usually too specific. Overly specific plans introduce an element of rigidity into the planning process that inhibits change and discourages accommodations to new conditions or to existing factors that have been overlooked.

A properly designed plan—a truly general plan—would be broad in scope and dimension. It would not be too precise in pinpointing uses proposed for specific lots or parcels of land. It would identify a number of transitional areas where change could be facilitated; it would permit judgments on particular land uses to be made after all pertinent matters relating to specific land uses were considered; and it would refrain from dictating for all time final decisions on land use. A good plan will avoid forcing future development decisions into a straitjacket, will encourage flexibility in future land-use decision-making, and will allow adjustment in future development policy to accommodate new and emerging land-use and social pressures. Plans should not cast the future of urban areas into concrete; unfortunately, they frequently do. Even though plans do not have the force of law, they nevertheless can shape significantly future development decisions.

Plans too often are little more than conventional maps depicting the planned future use of all land in the jurisdiction. This can have especially disastrous consequences for the suburban community, where much land commonly still remains undeveloped or in nonurban use. Under these circumstances, the plan may be viewed as a zoning ordinance that presumably will go into effect sometime in the future, and this can pose problems. For example, this approach can play havoc with land prices by adding to the land market an element of uncertainty that would not be present without a detailed plan. If the plan is not based on a realistic assessment of the growth requirements of the locality, and is overly specific, it may serve to stymie and artificially impede development.

Plans Do Not Serve Broad
Community Needs

Plans should be based on a broad conception of community needs. Plans frequently are not related to the community's need for varied and new land uses. Subarea plans are particularly guilty in this respect. Plans too often assume no change, and at best they only extend present uses. They too often are founded on the assumption that additional development is undesirable. The status quo must be preserved at all costs, and the plan is a chief means to this end.

Planning is intended to add an element of rationality to land development and community growth--an element that is not guaranteed by the "invisible hand" of Adam Smith. Planning is designed to sharpen the workings of the free marketplace. There is no inconsistency between the principles of private enterprise and planning. Planning is needed to guide and control development and to structure future land-use activity. Planning should not, however, stop development, halt growth, or stand in the way of expansion and progress. Plans far too commonly do just this.

Communities have many needs, and these needs may change and expand with time. Plans that are based on a narrow view of community needs, or on the idea that needs are static and limited, are inadequate. Plans that are predicated on the assumption that the community and the metropolitan area are not changing are unreasonable. To meet the community's responsibilities to its citizens, to the metropolitan area of which the community is but one part, and to the state and nation, plans should provide for orderly change, not seek to stop it. Communities do not exist unto themselves. They are part of a larger society, and this cannot be overlooked in the planning process.

This problem is especially significant in the case of sub-jurisdiction or area master plans. It is quite difficult to develop the broader perspective in these plans because there is a tendency to build into them the views and preferences of the most vocal and outspoken existing interests in affected neighborhoods. Too often, neighborhood interests of this variety do not take into account the overall needs of the community, city, county, or metropolitan area to which they belong, and they are apt to have no qualms about overriding compelling areawide needs for such land uses as low- and moderate-income housing and efficient regional transportation systems. The resulting plans may not even serve the immediate and private interests of the neighborhoods for which they are intended, as the dominant interests are likely to oppose needed public facilities and shopping areas. Planning that is only narrowly responsive to the interests of tiny areas cannot be true to its objectives. The more the narrow aims of neighborhood spokesmen are reflected in master plans the less chance the plan has of serving the public good.

Planning that is based on a static concept of the community, planning that does not provide systematically for productive change, and planning that does not encourage mixtures of land uses and residential densities cannot work in the interests of anyone over the long run. Planning should be a dynamic matter; it should be built on physical, social, and economic change. Planning should facilitate movement, progress, and growth. Neighborhood master plans often serve the opposite ends.

The purposes of a plan are to alert public authorities to future public and private facility and service needs as well as to the future requirements for residential uses. Public facilities and services include recreation and park areas, public safety buildings such as fire and police stations, sewage and water services, governmental administrative offices, highways, public utility uses, health centers, libraries, and other public activities and operations. Private facilities and services include shopping centers and areas, commercial office complexes, and private service establishments such as gas stations, real estate offices, and repair and maintenance outlets.

Determinations of the location of certain public facilities may have to conform to community master plans or to be reviewed by local planning and zoning authorities, while planning and land-use policy will determine what private services will be permitted in a community and where they will be located. Planning can have a meaningful influence over public and private facilities.

Local government must see to it that the necessary land is set aside for future public and private needs. This task is all the more difficult since needs clearly change with conditions and with the character of the population. Plans should take into account these needs and the changing conditions affecting them. Plans that assume no change, or that call for the extension of existing resi-

dential uses without considering future private and public
facility needs, do not perform the function they should.
They do not help public officials foresee future demands,
nor do they help officials meet these demands in an orderly
fashion. They do not encourage sound fiscal and administrative planning, and they do not permit the realization
of economic gains that can result from advance planning and
acquisition.

Plans Serve Class Ends

The master plan commonly serves as a class instrument
by which unwanted segments of the population are excluded,
and this is done by the use of the most legitimate and professionally worthy of tools. If the plan is essentially a
photograph of existing uses and their extension, and if the
area being served by the plan is middle to upper-middle
class in social structure, it is entirely possible that the
master plan is being used in this manner. It is just these
areas, particularly upper-middle-class neighborhoods, that
press local authorities to get into the sub-jurisdiction
master plan act, presumably for the purpose of promoting
economic class ends. Regardless of the motives, the results
have been clear.

When this pattern is repeated from community to community, from suburb to suburb, the master plan becomes but
another means by which the disadvantaged are kept in their
place at the bottom of the economic ladder, deprived of
the opportunity to mix with people without their handicaps,
and again sentenced to reside in ghettos. Through the
plan, the affluent are isolated from all but members of
their own economic class; and the children of the rich as-
sociate only with other children of similar economic background. This is not the America that is discussed in introductory political science texts; this is not the America
that we are taught about in the classrooms. But it is an
America that exists--an America that is dictated by the
suburban master plan.

How are economic class ends incorporated into master
plans? Plans calling for extensive large-lot development
and low-density residential use serve this purpose. So
do plans that prohibit apartments and diversity in land
use, plans that do not provide for low- and moderate-income
housing, and plans that severely restrict commercial, business, and industrial activity. These are all means by
which economic class homogeneity is promoted. Plans con-

46

taining such provisions are exclusionary and discriminatory. The primary effect is economic, although there may be social and racial implications as well.

Even within the middle and upper-middle classes, the master plan has become a chief vehicle by which further, more refined class distinctions are made and corresponding residential living patterns enforced. Plans quite often serve to stigmatize apartment development, particularly high-rise units, and to discriminate against high-density residential use of any type (regardless of the economic class served). The portion of the suburban middle class that so commonly stands behind the master plan appears to have an intense dislike of apartments, and this position all too frequently finds its way into the planning process, ultimately serving as the justification for zoning that does not permit high-density residential uses. Apartment dwellers are in effect designated second-class citizens and assigned a lower status in the internal social hierarchy of the middle class. Apartment residents are simply not wanted by many in the suburbs, and this view often becomes the foundation of the community master plan; apartments are considered undesirable, as are those who reside in them. It might be added that the anti-apartment stance is not without its ethnic or religious overtones--that is, in addition to the class factor.

This suggests that planning is not keeping up-to-date, that it is not keeping up with the times. This is not because communities do not have the required professional staff, or because we do not have the power to do what has to be done, or because there is no interest in planning on the part of the citizens, but because the concepts going into plans are not based on a realistic assessment of the world. No matter how hard we may try there is no practical way of retreating from change, no way of insulating ourselves in cozy neighborhoods inhabited by a single economic class and with walls protecting us from the larger universe around us. Unfortunately, many have operated as though they viewed the master plan as a means to this end, and in a manner reminiscent of medieval practice, they have sought through the plan to construct barriers that serve to isolate them from the outside world. We have found that this sort of policy does not work at the national or state level, but we are intent on making it work in our residential communities. Although this policy probably cannot be successful at the local level in the long run, one must concede that it is somewhat effective at present and may become more effective with the passing of each day--effective, that is, in the exclusionary sense.

Plans Do Not Adequately Protect
Open Space

In many instances, much of the land in the suburbs is undeveloped or not used for urban purposes. It is not uncommon for 75 to 90 percent of the suburban land area to be essentially undeveloped—to be used for farming, forestry and the like, or to be simply unused. Nationally, in 1960 less than 26,000 of the 310,000 square miles of land area in metropolitan areas were urbanized; and these figures include central cities as well as suburbs, suggesting that the suburbs were even less urbanized than these statistics indicate.

In treating nonurbanized and undeveloped land, master plans recently have taken the tack that this land should be placed in large-lot usage. Although a plan cannot dictate in the legal sense how land is to be used, it can generally point toward the kind of zoning needed to carry out the objectives of the plan. Large-lot development governed by large-lot zoning commonly is seen as a key means of keeping land in an undeveloped or basically rural or open-space use. No zoning category exists that would guarantee that land would not be developed at all, and zoning land for high minimum residential lot sizes has been considered the most logical way to inhibit and limit development and to preserve large areas designated as open space on the master plan.

Large-lot zoning affects land use in two basic ways: first, it means that any development that takes place will be limited to one house to one acre, or to two, three, four, five, or ten acres, depending on the minimum lot size found in the zoning ordinance and, second, that it will divert potential development from areas placed in the large-lot class to areas permitting houses on smaller lots, or more broadly, to areas of higher-density zoning. The economics of land use tends to lead developers to search for land that does not have high minimum lot-size requirements, for this means that more homes can be built, that economies of scale will allow for lower construction costs, that the cost of individual lots will be less, and that a much broader market can be reached.

Large-lot zoning is covered in greater detail in the next chapter, but suffice it to say here that it has by no means been an effective device by which to conserve open space. Plans may call for open spaces to serve as buffers between concentrations of development, working to channel urban uses into designated areas, or they may want open space saved for other purposes. Whatever the reason, open spaces have not been kept free of development.

Plans based on the open-space concept have been singularly unsuccessful in achieving their objectives. The land areas in the open-space wedges are not only being developed but also they are being developed in a way (as we can now see) that is not compatible with the goals of open-space planning. Even if one could consider large-lot development to represent open-space usage, the space that is preserved is located around each house and its use is limited to the residents of that house. It is not public but private open space, and much of it cannot even be seen by those who do not own land and homes in such areas. In the final analysis, this type of open space is bound to remain open only on planning maps and not in reality.

The conservation of open space, green areas, trees, and natural resources is essential. Given the pressures in the metropolitan area for more land, housing, and urban uses, would it not make more sense to plan for varied and mixed uses throughout the suburbs, retaining significant areas of open space around and near cluster developments containing different residential densities and lot sizes, as well as attractive commercial and shopping facilities? In this manner, urban uses will flow naturally with the environment, and close-by concentrations of open space can be enjoyed by all and will remain truly free of development. Plans can be designed to achieve these ends, and if they were we could attain the objectives that open-space wedges are supposed to attain, along with others that cannot be attained with traditional land-use control measures like large-lot zoning. Techniques presently are available to move us in this direction; these are discussed in Chapters 3 and 6.

It seems that plans that foresee setting aside huge chunks of open space are unrealistic. They are founded on the assumption that we already have enough close-in sections in the metropolitan area that can serve the need for high-density development. It is true that there is much land in the suburbs that remains undeveloped, but it is equally true that this land is not necessarily located where it could easily be used for needed housing, commercial, or other purposes. There is considerable pressure on virtually all land that is within a reasonable distance of work, shopping, offices, and industrial establishments. Most of the land area that is typically designated as open space on master plans, and that is zoned in the large-lot categories, probably falls into this class; it is land that could be used for housing people who need to live in decent homes near their jobs, or for other urban purposes equally consistent with overall community needs. If this land were developed as suggested here, much of it, perhaps most of it, could be conserved in its natural state. Effective development of land does not preclude protection of the environment or the conservation of natural features.

Another assumption that appears to be underlying plans with major concentrations of open space is that population can be controlled, that population growth and continued development can be stopped, and that all of this can be done at the community level. Of course, there is going to be a certain degree of population control wherever there are land-use regulations, but this control need not be exercised in the direction of limiting population expansion or putting an end to population in-migration. But these are the goals that seem to be reflected in open-space planning, and in most instances they are not only undesirable in principle but unrealistic in practice. Again, it must be conceded that plans based on the premise that the population growth rate must be curtailed and development halted may prove effective in the short run--that is, in achieving the intended antidevelopment end; much evidence can be cited suggesting indeed that this is precisely the case. One may legitimately ask, however, what right a suburban jurisdiction has to exclude others from locating within its borders. Even if the current population control drives succeed in cutting population growth rates, there still is going to be population movement, and this movement will be found within the metropolitan area as well as across metropolitan-area lines. Even with no rise in national or areawide population, some localities will be under pressure to admit new residents and to permit new land uses. How can local jurisdictions rightfully stand up and say to the rest of the metropolitan area: stay out, you may not locate in our area, our undeveloped land is planned for open-space use. Ultimately, communities will not be able to uphold such policies when the pressures become too great for their plans and land-use controls to withstand. But in the meantime we are in trouble, and community after community is thumbing its nose at the residents of other portions of the metropolitan area, a policy that particularly affects the poor, minorities, and nonwhites.

LOCAL DEMOCRACY AND PLANNING POLICY

What has been said so far raises some serious questions about the workings of democracy at the local level in America today. It should be recalled that our primary concern in this book is with the communities that are doing the most in planning, and these are the more affluent sections of the typical metropolitan area, generally the suburbs.

How are metropolitan areas and particularly the suburbs carved up for governmental purposes? How is planning administered in the metropolitan political system? The answer is simple: governmental and planning powers are highly localized and decentralized throughout the metropolitan area; basic planning and development decisions are made jurisdiction by jurisdiction, and presumably a majority of the residents of each jurisdiction make the planning decisions for particular areas. In the suburbs, planning decisions are commonly made by governments that have authority over a relatively small land area and that serve a relatively small population.

At last count, there were nearly 21,000 units of local government in metropolitan areas--an average of 91 governments per metropolitan area. A majority of the municipalities and townships (both may exercise planning authority) in metropolitan areas have populations of less than 5,000, and many local governments in metropolitan areas are responsibile for a land area covering less than 25 square miles. In some parts of the country, planning determinations are made in political subdivisions that have larger populations and more land area than this. The assignment of the planning function, of course, follows the general pattern of local government. In the South, for example, local government structure is less fragmented than in most other sections of the nation, and this stems from early colonial practice. In the South, planning is commonly a responsibility of local governments serving a larger land area and population than is typical elsewhere.[9] Nevertheless, within the metropolitan areas throughout the country, planning decisions are being made by minority interests; the only difference from one area to another is how small this minority is.

This, then, is the nature of the democracy that we have in planning in the United States. It is not sufficient to say that democratic practices surround the development and administration of planning policy in this country; it is not enough to say that the majority rules. One has to go behind these broad generalizations and inquire what this

51

democracy is in reality and what this majority is a majority of. If we are told that the people make planning decisions, we have every right to ask how these people are counted, and who these people are.

It is an unusual theory of democracy that says that however one counts the majority, it should rule. The larger metropolitan areas of the nation contain well over a million residents each; and the planning decisions in these areas are not made by a majority of the people in these areas taken as a whole, but by different minorities, perhaps by majorities of these minorities. Although it is not clear to what extent the people in each jurisdiction actually participate in the planning decision-making processes, it is clear that in most cases most of the residents of the metropolitan area are excluded from specific planning decisions. The specific planning decisions are made by particular subareas, by particular governmental units, by particular neighborhoods, or by minorities, usually small ones at that. The residents of the highly populated central cities have no voice whatsoever in suburban planning, nor do most suburban residents control specific planning decisions made in the suburbs (these decisions are made by particular segments of the suburban population).

Perhaps it would be possible to justify this brand of democracy if each political subdivision was self-sufficient, if each subdivision could support itself, if each jurisdiction could "go it alone." But this is not the kind of world we live in, and it is not reflective of reality in the metropolitan area. The various parts of the metropolitan area are highly interdependent, and, more important, they are interdependent in the land-use and development field. The suburban municipalities, townships, and counties are dependent on other portions of the metropolitan area in certain respects, as the city is dependent on the suburbs. Any major decision in planning and many minor ones can have a significant effect on the metropolitan area as a whole, or on particular sections of the metropolitan area outside the locality making the decision. Planning and land-use determinations are apt to have wide-ranging implications, and it is most unlikely that the effects of these determinations will be limited to a single political subdivision.

In fact, it seems reasonable to argue that in the long run planning and land-use decisions are among the most important ones that a society can make. That planning and land-use decisions do not receive the public visibility and attention that would be commensurate with their actual

significance does not weaken the point. What could be more
important than decisions that determine where a person will
live, the social class composition of the neighborhood in
which he will reside, the public facilities that will be
made available to him, the nature of the amenities to be
found in his environment, the location of places of business, the quality of the physical environment, the character of the transportation system, and the like? In America,
we have given the power to make such decision to thousands
of local governments, spread unevenly across the land and
subject to influences that are not necessarily compatible
with the public interest, no matter how that is defined.

There is no question that planning powers are not
properly distributed in the American political system.
Yet, as was said earlier, it appears that no basic restruc-
turing of power in the planning field is likely, politically
speaking. It seems, therefore, that we have no choice but
to work generally within the current governmental arrangements in planning. But at the same time any number of pressures can be effectively brought upon local authorities to
change the planning picture, at least to some extent.
There is nothing wrong with local governments, local minorities, local majorities of minorities, or even neighborhoods
making planning decisions so long as the decisions are consistent with the interests of the broader universe. The
interests of the broader universe of which the locality is
a part cannot be overlooked; these interests should be taken
into account in the local planning decision-making process.

METROPOLITAN INSTITUTIONS AND PLANNING

It would be wise to consider the creation of areawide
general-purpose metropolitan governments of a municipal
type that would do both metropolitanwide planning and set
planning and land-use decision-making standards for local
governments in the metropolitan area. This would be a step
in the right direction. The federation form of metropolitan government lends itself to this sort of arrangement;
and, under federation, the basic decisions in community development could continue to be made at the municipal and
suburban level. Through a metropolitan federation, it is
likely that metropolitanwide needs would be taken into account in planning decision-making and that localities could
not unilaterally establish planning policy that serves
purely exclusionary, antidevelopment, or upper-middle-class
ends. But metropolitan government is in the distant future
at best for most metropolitan areas.

In the meantime, we should seek to have metropolitanwide planning commissions and metropolitan councils of
government make local planning and community development
decision-makers aware of their responsibility to consider
the needs of the metropolitan area as a whole as well as
the legitimate interests of their own communities. This
means that local authorities should be persuaded to accept
residents of different income levels, to provide housing
in different price brackets, to encourage mixture and variety in land uses and residential densities, and to set
aside locations for needed commercial and business uses--
in short, to become full partners in the areawide scheme
of things. We should ask that an end be put to residential
class isolation, economic discrimination, social group and
racial segregation, urban sprawl, or at least to the planning practices that cause or contribute to these conditions.

Most of the nation's metropolitan areas now are engaged
to some extent in metropolitanwide planning and have some
form of metropolitanwide planning organization. Progress
has been made recently in the development of a continuing,
comprehensive transportation planning process at the metropolitan level. This process, which involves state highway
agencies and community officials, is to provide for the
metropolitanwide coordination of all aspects of transportation planning and the linking of transportation with land-
use planning. This may be one of the earliest practical
efforts to bring the metropolitan perspective to bear on
both community land-use planning and state highway planning.
The metropolitan transportation planning process began of-
ficially in 1965, and it is an experiment that bears watch-
ing.[10]

FEDERAL GOVERNMENT AND PLANNING

The federal government should be another source of
pressure on local planning authorities. The federal government is supported by all of the people of the United States,
as are the many urban project grant and loan programs funded
by Washington. As taxpayers and citizens of the nation,
we have every right to insist that our national government
not be a party to exclusionary and discriminatory planning
and that federal officials do everything within their power
to see to it that such activities are brought to a halt.

The national government provides considerable aid to
local governments, sometimes through the states and sometimes directly. Through the federal assistance programs,

the national authorities could require recipient communities to begin exercising their planning powers for the
benefit of the population generally, to plan as part of a
larger metropolitan area, to mix their land uses and open
their doors to varied development patterns, to begin planning for low- and moderate-income residents, to tear down
walls built by the planning mechanism, and to join the
broader American mainstream. Is this too much to expect?
We think not. It is our opinion that Washington will have
to act, and to act decisively. It would clearly be unwise
for the federal government to rule the communities, but
incentives and guides need to be established to push the
communities in the right direction.

STATE PLANNING

State planning has been considered by some as an alternative to present arrangements.* Although state governments
can be helpful in certain respects, it does not appear that
their assumption of the planning power would be the answer
to our problems. The state governments have done little
in this area in the past, and nothing suggests that they
will do more in the future. Besides, it is not likely
that decisions would be much if at all different with a
shift of planning from the local to the state level. This
reasoning would apply to the planning-related powers of
zoning and subdivision regulation as well.

NOTES

1. Lewis Mumford, The City in History (New York:
Harcourt, Brace & World, 1961).
2. Edward C. Banfield, The Unheavenly City (Boston:
Little, Brown, 1970), especially chap. 2. This book has
stirred much controversy, largely because of its unorthodox
and allegedly "conservative" character.
3. The President's Committee on Urban Housing makes
this point in relation to proposals that the United States
use Western European or Russian building systems. See A
Decent Home, The President's Committee on Urban Housing
(Washington, D.C.: Government Printing Office, 1969), p. 211.

---

*State planning will be discussed in some detail in
the Epilogue.

4. Daniel P. Moynihan, <u>Maximum Feasible Misunderstanding</u> (New York: The Free Press, 1969), p. 191.

5. As Grodzins suggests, "A detailed analysis would show that any division of functions, on the line of their 'local' or 'national' character, would leave precious few activities in the local category." See Morton Grodzins, "Why Decentralization by Order Won't Work," in Edward C. Banfield, ed., <u>Urban Government</u> (New York: The Free Press, 1961), p. 126.

6. Alexander Hamilton, James Madison, and John Jay, <u>The Federalist Papers</u> (New York: The New American Library, 1961); <u>Federalist</u>, No. 10, pp. 77-84.

7. General information on metropolitan government is found in <u>Alternative Approaches to Governmental Reorganization in Metropolitan Areas</u>, Advisory Commission on Intergovernmental Relations (Washington, D.C.: Government Printing Office, 1962). On differences in central city and suburban votes on metropolitan government proposals, see <u>Factors Affecting Voter Reactions to Governmental Reorganization in Metropolitan Areas</u>, Advisory Commission on Intergovernmental Relations (Washington, D.C.: Government Printing Office, 1962), especially p. 26.

8. Information on the occupational backgrounds of planning board members in the past can be found in: Robert A. Walker, <u>The Planning Function in Urban Government</u> (Chicago: University of Chicago Press, 1950), especially pp. 150-52; and Donald H. Webster, <u>Urban Planning and Municipal Public Policy</u> (New York: Harper & Row, 1958), especially p. 104.

9. In the South, key local powers, including planning, typically are found in county governments. In the Southern colonies, both the church (Anglican) and the political system at the local level tended to be centralized. This is to be contrasted with the early church (Puritan) and local government organization pattern in New England, in which power was highly localized. The country in general appears to have followed the New England lead. Alan Pendleton Grimes, <u>American Political Thought</u> (New York: Holt, Rinehart and Winston, 1960), p. 24.

10. For a discussion of the metropolitan transportation planning process and the links between transportation and land-use planning, see David E. Boyce and Norman D. Day, <u>Metropolitan Plan Evaluation Methodology</u> (Philadelphia: Institute for Environmental Studies, University of Pennsylvania, 1969).

3

ZONING IS NUMBER ONE

In the United States, an interest in planning is likely
to turn shortly to an interest in zoning. What is fascinating about zoning is that it is so widely criticized in
the planning profession and at the same time given such
limited attention in the planning texts. Zoning is sometimes pictured as just one of the many tools available to
planners; it is seldom viewed as one of the more effective
of these tools. It is, in fact, often considered to be
downright ineffective. But this assessment should not lead
observers as it sometimes leads professional planners to
the conclusion that zoning is powerless, that zoning has no
meaning. On the contrary, zoning is one of the most significant powers in the hands of governmental authorities
in this country. One can think of few public activities
that are as important, particularly in terms of its effects
on the community, the metropolitan area, and the nation.

WHAT IS ZONING?

It is not the plan that determines how land will be
used, it is zoning. Zoning comes first, and planning is
placed in a subordinate position; this is true in a number
of different ways.

Technically, zoning is a land-use control, like subdivision regulations and the official map. Zoning is one
means that governments use to regulate private land and
building development within their jurisdictions. It is an
example of the exercise of the police power of the state,

which is usually delegated to local governments. Typically, states adopt enabling legislation permitting municipalities and perhaps other local governments to perform the zoning function; local governments also may be empowered to undertake zoning through home-rule charters. Ultimately, zoning is made law through the adoption of a zoning ordinance by the local government, and it is the local government that becomes the administering unit.

The zoning ordinance is made law by enactment by the local governing body, which may amend it as well. The zoning ordinance will contain a text and a map, the former being the written part, which stipulates the particular districts or zones of land use permitted and the restrictions and regulations that apply to these districts, and the latter being the pictorial layout, which shows the legally stipulated use of each lot and piece of land regulated by the ordinance. The use of land as designated on the zoning map is not necessarily the same as the actual use of the land; the legally stipulated zoning for particular lots cannot be determined simply by looking at the land, but by consulting the zoning map. In addition, the zoning map should not be confused with the planning map; the latter specifies desired, not necessarily legally stipulated, use.

According to conventional practice, the three categories of land use in the zoning ordinance were: residential (usually single-family), commercial, and industrial. As time passed, there has been a tendency for communities to develop additional categories and to subdivide the existing categories into a number of classes with more specific stipulations and refinements (this was done from the start in many localities). There is a current trend toward the adoption of zoning categories that allow for the mixture of land uses, particularly residential with commercial. Although the practice is not too widespread, the present emphasis on mixed uses is a departure from the conventional method of fully separating land uses, especially isolating residential from other sections of town. There also has been a recent tendency for zoning ordinances to permit more varied layout patterns and, to some extent, density mixtures in residential zones. Zoning customarily has required highly structured and predetermined layout patterns as well as separation of different residential densities.

ZONING: THE FOUNDATION OF
SUBURBAN POLITICS

Much of what is printed in the metropolitan and suburban newspapers about land-use activity in outlying residential neighborhoods revolves around zoning--usually proposed rezonings. Upon the adoption of the zoning ordinance, the local government will apply particular sections of the ordinance to the land area within its boundaries. This is done on the basis of the public officials' understanding of the needs and feelings of the community, and it is often premised on rather short-range perspectives, if indeed much thought goes into the process at all. Legally, of course, the general welfare, safety, health, and morals of the people serve as the basis for zoning decision-making.

With time, new pressures for land change develop, and conditions may not be the same as they were when the land was originally zoned. It also is possible that the land was not zoned properly in the first place. But, for whatever reason, once the owner of a particular piece of land decides that the existing zoning is not appropriate for that land, he may seek a rezoning.

A rezoning is technically a change in the zoning map, but its purpose is to provide for new use of the land. Commonly, land for which a rezoning is requested is unused or undeveloped, but sometimes the land already has improvements on it, including buildings or homes. Most rezonings are initiated by landowners or their representatives; until recently, it has not been common for the municipality or the planning board to initiate the rezoning of particular tracts without a request from the owner. Rezoning applications are typically in response to pressures of the marketplace for more intensive use of land, or for a change from one category of use to another for which there is a demand. Normally, a rezoning of land at the request of the owner will have the effect of raising the value of that land, for the new use is likely to allow for a greater residential density or for commercial activity, both of which are apt to command a higher economic return.

Not infrequently, rezonings are requested for a change from a single-family residential to a higher-density residential or to a commercial category. It is precisely here where rezoning applications become hotly contested politi-

cal issues. This is the crux of land-use politics in the
suburbs, and suburban land-use politics is commonly the
base of general politics in the suburbs. Basic conflict
in the suburbs is often over rezonings, and rezonings are
big business to all concerned.

The battle lines are clearly drawn: on the one hand,
there are those attempting to serve market needs, those
working for change in community development, those seeking
to accommodate new residents and business, those wanting
the highest economic use of and return from the land, those
wighing to rezone land; and, on the other hand, there are
those who oppose change in land use, those who want existing patterns preserved, those who are sensitive to the interests of neighborhoods that want new land uses and residents excluded, those who bitterly fight rezonings. The
first set of forces is sometimes unorganized in the formal
sense, although it may be represented by local builder-
developer associations; the second often is represented by
neighborhood citizens groups. Both of these sets of forces
are likely to possess considerable political clout by which
to back up their interests. Both have important economic
stakes in zoning--the builders, their profits; citizens
groups, their home values.

ZONING IS A CLASS MATTER

Zoning is essentially a middle-class and upper-middle-
class matter, even more so than planning. Further, zoning
traditionally has been a homeowner's matter, the concern
of the homeowner who has a house on a separate lot. Regardless of what zoning may be in theory, in practice it
has become the chief means of protecting and isolating the
single-family residence.[1] Zoning is considered by the homeowner to be the chief means by which he can protect his
residence, his neighborhood, and his home investment. Not
all homeowners see things this way, but enough do to cause
the view to be translated into political reality.

One may ask what we are protecting the single-family
residence from. The answer is that we are protecting it
from virtually any land use that the most vocal of the
single-family residents do not consider desirable. This
includes industrial uses (especially), most if not all commercial uses, residential uses for low- and moderate-income
families, high-density residential uses including high-
rise apartments (particularly) and garden or low-rise apartment units (in most cases), perhaps townhouse uses, certain

kinds of public uses and facilities (main highways, public safety facilities).

Probably the most dreaded land use is homes for low-income persons or for families with incomes lower than those of the present residents; even housing for moderate-income families assisted under government programs is feared and viewed as a serious threat to the economic stability of the neighborhood.

Neighborhoods commonly are organized to make sure that zoning is used in the "proper" manner--that is, to protect single-family areas from unwanted uses. Neighborhood citizens associations often will bring much pressure to bear on public officials to make zoning decisions that are compatible with this conception. The public official who is not sensitive to these arguments is subject to citizens group censure and is apt to be punished at the next election.

The delightful part about this--from the citizens group point of view--is that zoning can be used by middle- and upper-income neighborhoods in this manner without bringing the wrath of the moralists down on them. This also applies to planning, as we saw in Chapter 2, but zoning is the real power behind planning; and it is zoning that gives teeth to planning ideals and objectives. Planning as such cannot require that land be used in a particular manner, but zoning can. One cannot avoid the impression that planning comes after zoning when a community is really serious about keeping others out. That is, planning simply provides legitimacy to the zoning preferences and biases of the community.

In reality, a community could disregard planning if it had the zoning authority, and it appears that many do just that. (It is no accident that more metropolitan area municipalities have zoning ordinances than planning boards; it is also interesting that the federal government first issued its model zoning-enabling legislation years before it released its model planning-enabling legislation.) But other communities, probably most, would find it far too uncouth to blatantly disregard planning--this would be going too much to the heart of the matter, striking a direct blow for economic segregation, class exclusiveness, ethnic discrimination, religious intolerance, and racial purity.

It would openly assure that the children in the community would not have to come into contact with poor people, with people of different races and religious beliefs, or with their children. It would be announcing to one and all that they consider their class to be supreme, their background superior, their values higher. No, this would not be acceptable. Communities want exclusive neighborhoods and all the discrimination this implies--but they want them dressed up in a community plan, a plan that calls for single-family dwellings on medium- to large-sized lots with private open space. Then zoning--the behind-the-scenes power, the power that does not merit even a single chapter in any of the leading planning texts--is trotted out and put to work. Nothing else is foolproof. Zoning is king-- and it is no less ruthless than the monarchs we read about in history books. It serves class ends, it serves an elite, it is used to advance the interests of the few.

Moralists concentrate their fire on business, on developers, on real estate speculators, on capitalism. Not that everything is all right in these areas, but what about zoning? What about the use of government power to underwrite the preferences of a single class, of the single-family homeowner? Do we not have every right to question this practice? Is all the blame for urban ills to be placed on the business community? Or can it be placed elsewhere, perhaps even more justifiably, on practices and institutions the moralists have been taught to respect? What prominent liberal white has spoken out against suburban zoning practices? What prominent white clergyman has criticized the zoning ordinances used to isolate middle-income and upper-income single-family neighborhoods from the poor? Or is it that by drawing attention to matters of secondary importance one can keep the poor, the disadvantaged of any race, from looking at the real problem?

The real problem is zoning. We cannot solve a single one of our other domestic problems without launching a direct attack on community zoning. Any assertion to the contrary is misleading and stems from an absence of understanding of the roots of community development.

ZONING AND POLITICAL IDEOLOGY

Liberalism and conservatism both address themselves to current problems and policies. Neither, however, seems to be of much practical value in correcting our urban development ills.

One must seriously question the approach typically used by liberals to battle social injustice. One must question the value of liberalism when it is applied selectively to the issues of the day, and one must wonder to just what extent this philosophy in its most fundamental

sense serves to protect and promote the status quo. In
any event, the protection of the status quo seems to be the
effect of liberalism; the preservation of existing patterns
of social and physical development is the product of liberalism, no matter what may be its intent. And again, these
patterns are preserved in the most reputable of ways. The
young, the students, and the naive of all ages think highly
of anyone who takes a liberal stand on issues that are re-
mote from us, on matters that do not affect their economic
interests, on general policies, on abstractions. It is
fine to support the admission of Red China into the United
Nations so long as we do not have to admit the poor into
our neighborhoods. It is fine to support integration of
the schools in the South so long as we do not have to integrate our neighborhoods in the North. It is fine to support
public housing in principle so long as we do not have to
put up with it ourselves. In this manner, one can reap the
intangible and image-building benefits of appearing to be
broad-minded and generous without personally having to be
threatened with change. In fact, nothing important to us
is affected at all. A big question mark can be placed on
the effectiveness of the upper-middle-class liberal idealism
that is so common in this country.[2]

By the same token, one cannot be happy with the way
conservatism has been practiced either. Do not conservatives
claim to favor the impartial and limited exercise of government power everywhere? But where is the philosophical conservative when it comes to exposing restrictive zoning practices, when it comes to condemning the use of government
power to keep one class or race of people out of an area?
How consistent is it to rail against the overuse of government authority at the national level and to back economically
and racially discriminatory zoning actions of government at
the local level? Some members of the middle and upper classes complain that the government is being run for the benefit of the blacks, the poor, or other minorities. They
frequently point out the high taxes they pay to support the
programs of welfare and social-action agencies. They reserve
special condemnation for politicians who are said to be op-
portunistically cultivating the black vote and the votes of
the poor whites and the young. These allegations invariably
are made by political conservatives who live in affluent
residential neighborhoods, the class structure and social
exclusiveness of which are sustained artificially not by
the laws of economics but by the zoning power of government.
If the poor are in fact benefiting from government welfare
programs, even to an unfair degree, are not the rich bene-

fiting at least to the same extent from government zoning
ordinances?

If the truth about zoning were known and we had the
guts to stand up and do something about it, much of the
fire now directed at the right wing would be aimed at the
suburbs. The right wingers draw this fire because they
have the nerve, and perhaps because they are unsophisticated
enough, to admit to beliefs that are highly unpopular and
that strike most people as being both evil and hopelessly
out-of-date. But this point should be made: the right
wing does not control our communities, our states, or the
nation. The values and views that we now attribute to the
political far right (racial prejudice, religious intolerance,
etc.) are practiced on a widespread basis in the suburbs,
though little is said about this. And it is the practice
of prejudice and intolerance that counts much more than the
adherence to the values supporting them. In many respects,
suburbanites are in the enviable position of being able to
shun these unpopular right-wing values--and even in effect
to condemn them by supporting liberal candidates, attending
liberal churches, talking a liberal line--while at the
same time translating these same values into practice through
restrictive zoning. Liberal action is stymied successfully
in the only area where it can be seen, understood, or have
any real meaning--in our own neighborhoods, where we live,
where we play, where we raise our children, where we spend
our time. So long as suburbanites cling to their exclusionary and antidevelopment zoning ordinances, the liberalism they may express must remain suspect if not downright
fraudulent.

ZONING IS RIGGED

It is clear that many domestic government programs do
not end up serving the intended clientele--and this is particularly true when the clientele are in the lower economic
levels. Zoning is supposed to serve all the people, yet
it often serves only particular interests, particular classes. In this sense, zoning can be equated with other government activities.

But in the case of zoning, the situation is more obvious and more serious, because so much of the population
is excluded from making decisions. Central city residents
play little or no role in suburban land-use matters, including zoning. A majority of the population in the nation's
metropolitan areas now resides in the suburbs; in some cases

the suburban population ranges as high as 75 percent or
more of the total metropolitan area population. At a recent
convention of county officials, the suburbs were described
as a coalition working against the interests of the city.
One can rest assured that this coalition would rapidly dis-
integrate if the suburbs were stripped of their zoning
power. Zoning holds the suburbs together, it props up social classes, it literally keeps the city out, and it ex-
cludes all of the influences of the city as well. Suburbanites still use the city for their own ends--for work,
business, entertainment, shopping--but the reverse is not
true.

　　While it is not uncommon for government programs to
work in a way that was not intended, in zoning the game
has been rigged from the beginning. In other words, it
was never intended that zoning be used for the people in
general. It was and is known that zoning will work for
the interests of those who have the power over it--and at
present those who have the power are normally the homeowners and their representatives in the suburbs. The suburbanites now have a stranglehold over zoning, and they are
determined to use it to protect their economic and social
interests.

　　One might argue that this state of affairs is not so
bad, that it is to be expected, and that it is a natural
development, given human propensities and economic realities. Regardless of this argument, the Constitution of the
United States guarantees all citizens equal protection under
the law, a provision that specifically applies to state
governments. As a power of the state granted to local political subdivisions, zoning falls within the scope of
this constitutional provision. Legally then, as well as
in other respects, zoning that is discriminatory, zoning
that is exclusionary, cannot be justified.

　　Zoning ordinances have different provisions, covering
different types of land use. Yet if zoning had only one
provision--that of stipulating single-family residences on
individual lots--it would still succeed in its basic aim.
One is led to speculate what caused the widespread interest
in zoning among reformers and others in the 1920s when it
was first introduced on any important scale in this country,
and what made so many people believe that it would bring a
new day in community development. As zoning has been used,
it has not brought this new day. It has served only one
end: the protection of the single-family dwelling from
"incompatible" uses. Far from being a positive force in
communities, it has been a negative one; it has been used

to defend the status quo, to hold the line.

Zoning is being used to stop change, not just to impede it--to put an end to change, not just to slow it a bit. It is a perversion of planning when localities can use it as the professional window dressing for status quo zoning. Communities are paying consultants, planning professionals, experts of all kinds to stamp the seal of approval on zoning practices founded on the narrowest of values and objectives.

ZONING: THE KEY LAND-USE INFLUENCE

The theory of planning holds that zoning is simply one of the possible tools that can be used to implement plans. In theory, it is not considered a particularly important tool. But zoning is just about the only realistic tool that communities have with which to carry out the objectives of planning, and this is so in spite of the fact that professional planners are taught that zoning is not all that useful, is not too effective, and is basically a holding action at best. Professional planners have little confidence in zoning and spend much time searching for alternatives. But it appears that the search is in vain, and that ultimately professional planners like others will conclude that zoning is really the most effective tool that exists for controlling development and land use; more important, they will discover that zoning is planning--that is, it represents the reality of planning. Communities do not really plan at all; they just zone--and that is the long and short of it. The plan serves the same purpose that liberalism does--it is the outer cover; zoning represents the reality of the situation.

The subdivision regulation and official map powers were mentioned above. Subdivision regulations are an important land-use control; they cover site design and layout, helping to assure that new developments of large tracts of land conform to the general existing or planned physical patterns in the area. Subdivision controls treat such matters as the public improvements (streets, sidewalks, sewers, etc.), fees, and dedications of land for certain public purposes to be provided by the developer. The official map is used by communities to reserve land and rights-of-way for future public needs (especially streets) and serves to keep these areas free of development. But neither subdivision controls nor the official map have the impact on the community that zoning does.

Zoning determines the basic pattern of development in the community, and subdivision controls must work within

the general frame established by zoning. Zoning determines
the fundamental pattern of use of private land, designating
minimum lot sizes, maximum densities, building setback
lines (from the street, other residences, buildings, lots),
height limitations, minimum house sizes, off-street parking
requirements, and permitted general uses. Once the zoning
ordinance is adopted and applied, the character of community
development is set and cannot be changed without a change
of zoning.

Still, other public activities have much to do with
shaping community development and growth patterns. These
include the building of roads, sewer and water lines, mass
transit systems, and the location of government buildings
and institutions. These activities are not under the jurisdiction of zoning, and yet they may independently affect
community development directions. Ideally, all public programs and facilities would be coordinated with zoning, perhaps through the planning process, but the fact is that
they are not. It is nevertheless zoning that determines
how private land near or affected by these activities will
be used. Although these public actions clearly influence
land-use patterns generally, zoning tells us precisely how
specific pieces of land will be used, and how they will be
developed. There is no way of avoiding zoning. It will
not go away, and it will most likely be the decisive land-
use force in the long run.

Zoning will have to be tapped by anyone interested in
molding land-use patterns, no matter what his objectives
might be. Although zoning is presently used to inhibit
change, it need not necessarily be used in this manner.
Zoning can be used for any purpose, to achieve whatever
end is set for it. The paragraphs to follow are dedicated
to detailing the weaknesses of present zoning practices.
After this, we turn to suggestions and techniques for
changing these practices.

WHAT'S WRONG WITH ZONING?

Zoning Is Antidevelopment

Most of the developed residential portions of the
outlying sections of the nation's metropolitan areas, both
inside and outside the central city, are zoned for small-
lot uses--that is, single-family residences on land parcels
of less than a quarter acre each, or certainly no more than
a quarter or half acre. This accounts for the dominant char-

acteristic of the contemporary middle- and upper-income residential area in the metropolis--a single-family house on a small, individual lot. These small-lot homeowners supply the political muscle behind zoning policy. But over the past ten years or so, these suburban residents have not been satisfied to provide newcomers with the same kind of small lots that the old residents have and, instead, have given their support to zoning in the larger-lot categories (one acre or more).

The reasons for this are undoubtedly mixed, but one of the most important has been the desire to keep the presently nonurbanized land in an essentially undeveloped state. This undeveloped land is commonly labeled "open space" on the plan, but often the motive behind putting open spaces on the plan in the first place is to prevent development. Large-lot zoning is used as a means to this end, since it presumably stops development. How large-lot zoning may serve to divert development is discussed in Chapter 2. Many suburbanites are reasonably open in admitting their opposition to further development, especially high-density residential or commercial development.

Large-lot zoning has not, in fact, kept open-space areas free of development as was apparently intended, although it has affected the nature of development in the community. Nor has it conserved open spaces as was expected. It has, however, contributed to urban sprawl and other problems, and it has had economic and fiscal implications at the community level. The discussion of large-lot zoning is continued in the next section.

Zoning Is Exclusionary

Many suburbanites oppose all new development, and large-lot zoning is a chief antidevelopment tool. Commercial development often is opposed in the suburbs as a matter of principle--it simply is not wanted, and no reason need be given. Of course, if all the available land is zoned large-lot residential, commercial uses of any kind are automatically excluded; that industrial uses are not wanted and excluded goes without saying. The reasoning of the typical suburbanite on residential development is a little more complex. If large-lot zoning can stop all development, this is fine, and zoning is achieving its objective. But it is also true that if there is to be development, suburbanites would rather it be such that only higher-income residents would be attracted. The point is that if land is zoned in large-lot categories, only estates and large homes will be built, and this sort of development is generally considered compatible with existing land-use patterns.

Now, why do so many suburbanites want only expensive homes and higher-class residents? Time and time again, one hears the familiar answer: Our objective is to keep taxes in line, to attract land uses that do not add to the tax burden of the community. Zoning for such ends is sometimes called fiscal zoning.

When, during 1965 and 1966, students at the University of Pennsylvania made systematic inquiries concerning Philadelphia's exclusive Mainline, suburban officials gave them the same unswerving response: large-lot zoning was done for tax purposes. Especially significant in this respect were educational outlays. That is, suburban decision-makers explained that zoning policy was formed with an eye toward maintaining current levels of school taxes, although other public services and facilities also were considered important in this sense. The argument is that new residents are costly to the community—new people mean more classrooms, more streets, more sewer and water extensions, more police, and so on. Zoning policy, it is held, should be directed toward keeping these costs and corresponding tax levels to a minimum.

To many officials interviewed, the ideal alternative seemed to be no new residents at all; thus, large-lot zoning that inhibits all development is best, and the larger the lot the better. Less than ideal but still acceptable solutions were lot-size minimums that assured development in the higher price ranges. Higher property values mean a higher tax assessment base, and this means more money for community coffers. By the same token, according to the officials, smaller lots lead in the opposite direction—that is, smaller assessable bases and lower tax contributions.

The point is that high-income residents and high-priced housing are supposed to put less pressure on community services and tax levels than alternative residential patterns. Since local governments draw more revenues from the property tax than any other single source, property values must be taken into account.[3] In addition, it is contended that higher density residential development is likely to mean that families with more children will come to the community, putting a major strain on the public school system, which usually consumes the better part of the property tax dollar. But no official interviewed even hinted that land-use policy might be shaped to exclude blacks, lower-income whites, or

69

to maintain a certain economic class level. No, this was
never the argument. The only points discussed had to do
with economics, with fiscal matters; the only arguments
were those that dealt with taxes and costs of public services and facilities. Even these points were theoretical,
inexact, and speculative--but they were the reasons given.

Fiscal zoning is, in fact, common in Philadelphia's
suburban areas, including the Mainline where the interviews
were conducted. A study published in the early 1960s by
the Fels Institute of Local and State Government at the University of Pennsylvania shows that nearly 50 percent of the
land area in that city's Pennsylvania suburbs was zoned for
minimum residential development of one acre per house.[4]
This study covered a large four-county area and found that
one of these counties had over two-thirds of its land area
zoned in the one-acre-or-more category of minimum lot size.
Zoning in the Philadelphia suburbs is an undertaking of
township governments, and particular townships were discovered to have zoned large portions of their land areas
in two- and four-acre minimums. Some townships had placed
virtually all of their land in large-lot minimums of one
acre or more. Since the Fels study was done, the available
evidence suggests that substantially more of the land area
in the outer reaches of this major Eastern metropolis now
is zoned in large-lot minimums, as township after township
has been busily "up-zoning" its territory. "Up-zoning"
refers to action raising residential lot-size minimums or
generally shifting land into large-lot and lower-density
residential categories. (Some communities refer to this
as "down-zoning," because of the fall in density.)

The game of fiscal zoning is being played on a nationwide basis. The National Commission on Urban Problems reports that fully one-quarter of the municipalities in metropolitan areas do not permit residential development on lots
of less than a half acre, that in Connecticut over half of
the residentially zoned land currently vacant is in one-
or two-acre minimum districts, that in suburban Geauga
County outside Cleveland more than four-fifths of the land
area zoned for residential use must be developed in one-
acre or more minimums, and that zoning of land to higher
lot-size minimums and to lower densities is a characteristic practice in the suburbs of different parts of the
United States.[5]

What is so notable and downright astonishing about
these trends is that as more and more Americans seek to
move to the suburbs, as more and more industry attempts to

leave the city for outlying areas, as the need for additional commercial outlets grows, and as the pressures on existing land in the suburbs escalate at galloping rates, suburban planners are actively removing huge chunks of land from the market. It does little good to suggest that plenty of land can be found near the metropolitan area and that suburban land therefore need not be made available to those who wish to use it for residential purposes, for the lower-middle-income whites and blacks who are excluded from the suburbs by this land-removal process cannot possibly commute from distant points to metropolitan area jobs. The same goes for business; a commercial establishment cannot be expected to leapfrog over the suburbs and locate its facilities where they are removed from its workers and customers.

Viewed from an overall metropolitan vantage point, the present zoning trends in the suburbs reflect a withdrawal from reality, a withdrawal, however, that does not only affect those isolating themselves from the metropolitan masses but others whose aspirations and income levels are just beginning to cause them to want to enjoy a new way of life outside congested cities. A recent study by Harvard professors and students found that low-income residents of Boston area ghettos wanted grass and trees near their homes more than anything else. The desire to live in the suburbs or at least in a suburban type of environment has not waned in recent years, and it may have risen somewhat.[6]

Some people who have no special philosophical, environmental, socioeconomic, or value-based reason for wanting to move to the suburbs are anxious to do so because that is where their jobs are. What of the thousands of schoolteachers, public servants at the middle and lower pay levels, and service-maintenance workers of all types who are employed in the suburbs--are they to be denied the right to live near their jobs because of suburban zoning policy? The fact is, intentionally or otherwise, the suburbs are denying them this right. The costs of such action for workers and employers are heavy--turnover is higher, job dissatisfaction is prevalent, low productivity is the rule, tardiness is frequent, and frustration is heightened. The toll on the community is high--unnecessary automobile use is generated, pollution of the air is greater, public service costs are higher, and tax revenues are lost.

Large-lot zoning is not the only kind that is exclusionary. Zoning land for single-family development only and the imposition of zoning restrictions requiring large

houses may have the same effect.* Single-family zoning, if
extended over a wide area, means the elimination of multiple-
dwelling units. Multiple-family dwellings cannot, of
course, be built in single-family-unit zoned areas. Multifamily housing may mean inexpensive housing, and this in
turn may serve to broaden the housing market. Single-
family zoning, especially large-lot zoning, is apt to mean
more expensive housing. Zoning can regulate housing size
by stipulating a minimum floor area (minimum square foot-
age). If too stringent, minimum house sizes alone may
raise the costs of building to a point where housing is
put out of the reach of families with modest means.

Other land-use control practices also may be exclusionary. Examples are zoning that bars mobile homes, and
unnecessarily demanding subdivision requirements. Zoning
ordinances explicitly may prohibit mobile homes or may impose certain restrictions on home building (such as minimum floor areas) that have the same effect. Mobile homes
commonly are available to persons of low and moderate incomes. Further, communities may add to the cost and price
of housing by requiring developers to make more than the
customary land and public improvements. The costs of these
improvements typically are borne by the developer and
can be expected to be passed along to the homebuyer in
the ultimate price of the house; this serves to restrict
the market to persons of means.

One cannot overstate the side effects of exclusionary
zoning and subdivision control practices. These practices
make attempted integration of the schools something less
than a serious endeavor, for it is the segregated residential patterns in most parts of the nation that cause segregation in the public schools. Because of zoning the 1954
Supreme Court integration decision[7] has become impossible
to implement in that it cannot be carried out short of
busing students all over town, a course of action that apparently is desired by neither the parents nor the students
of either race.

The cause of racially integrated housing cannot be advanced to any significant extent without changing present
zoning regulations. This is a view that is shared by key
leaders of the black and brown communities. The National
Association for the Advancement of Colored People (NAACP)
is now pressing the courts in several sections of the nation

_____

*Single-family zoning includes but is not limited to
large-lot residential zoning.

on this matter, charging that local land-use controls are being employed to keep blacks out of white residential neighborhoods, or at least that such controls have this effect. In Oyster Bay on Long Island in New York, for example, the NAACP wants the local government to rezone land from single-family to multifamily use, thus making room for minorities and the poor. Whether the laws are directly aimed at excluding Negroes is not the concern, spokesmen of the NAACP point out; it is only necessary to show that they have this effect. It is argued that exclusionary zoning is contrary to the 14th Amendment of the Constitution (the Equal Protection clause that applies to the states and their political subdivisions).

The National Committee Against Discrimination in Housing successfully protested municipal regulations in Union City, California; a federal court ruled that the locality has a constitutional duty to provide housing for the poor (in the Union City case, "the poor" were generally Mexican Americans). Similarly, the administration in Washington filed suit against Black Jack, Missouri, a St. Louis County suburb, seeking to overturn municipal action, which in effect zoned out blacks. In the celebrated Black Jack case, the area used zoning to incorporate or eliminate multifamily housing projects, and in this way blocked a planned federally subsidized housing development. The federal Department of Housing and Urban Development has applied fiscal sanctions to Warren, Michigan, for its discriminatory housing policies.

Furthermore, zoning as presently used has wide-ranging consequences in other' respects. Exclusionary zoning practices often contribute significantly to inefficient transportation systems, an excessively polluted central city and suburban environment, and higher-class dominance of local (suburban) government. The urban sprawl and inefficient land use caused by exclusionary zoning work against a sound transportation system and place too much of an emphasis on roads and automobiles; this in turn serves to undermine the quality of the environment, as the car is the greatest single source of air pollution.[8] By segregating the more fortunate economic classes from the others, exclusionary zoning assures higher-class dominance of many, perhaps most, governments in the typical metropolitan area.

It would be unrealistic to suppose that much social progress could be made without changes in local zoning ordinances, for it is these ordinances that set the stage for all varieties of social relationships in the metropolitan area. It is unlikely that current efforts in social welfare, poverty eradication, education of disadvantaged youth, and upgrading of the aspirations of the poor can succeed so long as the power of zoning is used the way it is. No one could possibly assess the adverse effects that zoning has had on the emotional health of individuals in different economic classes, particularly in view of the conflict that may be caused by exclusionary land-use policies in the minds of the affluent young. Sensitive young people know that the moral values they are taught in the home and school are not compatible with the social and physical environment in which they are raised, an environment that is structured in no minor way by zoning and land-use controls.

Costs of this kind are high to the community and to the nation. Unfortunately, they are costs that are not normally measured by our leading social analysts and academic institutions. It is, of course, possible to reverse these patterns, but this will not be done unless there is sufficient awareness of the effects of municipal land-use controls on those who are suffering from their administration. The action to change zoning will have to be backed by the young, the leaders of the black and brown communities, and by adult whites who can see the enormous price exclusionary zoning is exacting from all of us.

Zoning Discourages Diversity

Zoning, as presently practiced, does not encourage diversity, variety, or experimentation. It does not provide us with the amenities and the wide range of land uses that we want and need. In fact, zoning seems to be especially well-designed to assure the misuse of land; it promotes sameness and a routine monotony, unequaled in the history of man. And for what end? One is hard-pressed to come up with an answer, although the previous paragraphs may provide some clue.

Current practice in zoning has evolved with only slight if any periodic reexamination and reevaluation; we are victims of the status quo in zoning, as change is not automatically guaranteed in land-use controls any more than in any other policy field. It may be that local administration of zoning works against change, for whatever advantages may be associated with community control, there is a tendency for small areas not to renew themselves.[9] The tendency is for parochialism to reign supreme, for narrow values to prevail, and for outright oppression to go unchallenged. Clearly, zoning is in great need of infusions from the broader society, from the larger order of things.

One of the most conspicuous failures of suburban zoning ordinances can be seen in the endless rows of look-alike houses dotting the outlying metropolitan landscape. Nothing could be less appealing from an aesthetic point of view, and the absence of variety does not permit a proper blending of development styles into the environment. Even the sight of such neighborhoods is enough to cause one to question the whole value-structure supporting the single-family residence. One might argue that this pattern is dictated by builders who by constructing the same house time and time again or by using a few standard models can build at economies of scale. Given current zoning ordinances, this is quite true, but there is no reason why zoning regulations need read the way they do. So long as zoning requires one house per lot and permits nothing else, the building industry will work for the greatest uniformity possible, saving on construction costs so as to be able to charge lower prices and thereby attract the broadest possible segment of the home-buying market. Thus, builders and developers cannot be held entirely responsible for the condition of our suburban areas. Their actions are strictly regulated and constrained by local government, especially by zoning.

In so many suburban subdivisions built under conventional zoning regulations one sees no commercial establishments, no diversity in land uses, no changes in drab patterns and architectural styles, and no relief from the blandness in development. Zoning should permit and encourage variety--variety in construction methods, variety in population densities, variety in lot sizes, variety in the class character of the residents served. Perhaps there was a day when a psychological end was served by having the same structure on lot after lot, the same type of neighbors, the same layout of house after house, and the absence of private and public facilities of all sorts; but today one is led to question both whether such needs ever existed and whether this development pattern is at all compatible with the urgent requirements and values of the present age.

Much of the conventional zoning in this country is based on a Euclidian principle that development should proceed along neatly arranged rows and street patterns, with each house having the same front-yard, side, and rear-yard setbacks; the same lot size; and the same general architectural style. However pleasingly symmetrical this pattern may appear on paper, it looks perfectly atrocious in practice; however acceptable it may be theoretically, it is unacceptable in reality. For any number of reasons, it would

be better to allow greater freedom in building, greater
flexibility in layout and design, greater leeway in trying
new techniques. This sort of approach would permit experimentation with housing in different price ranges; if each
house did not have to have a large lot, a big back yard,
and wide side and front yards, some homes with less land
could be provided, and these homes would probably be less
expensive than those built under more restrictive regulations. The introduction of properly planned public facilities and appropriate commercial establishments into residential neighborhoods would serve useful ends, provide
needed variety, and allow an aesthetically attractive blending of different land uses with different aspects of the
environment.

We should take another look at the common practice of
zoning entire jurisdictions or broad sections of the community into a single-use category, again a typical suburban
phenomenon. Invariably, this single-use category is the
one-family residence on a separate lot, and the concept is
often carried to an unconscionable extreme. Why not have
zoning provide a mixture of townhouses, garden apartments,
and single-family dwellings within a single neighborhood?
Why not have land-use regulations permit the construction
of a local shopping facility, or a community commercial
and recreational center?

In areas for which more intensive development is suitable, it is reasonable to urge local authorities to zone
for properly planned office buildings, perhaps alongside
apartment houses. The advantages of this sort of land-use
pattern are numerous, and the most obvious of these are
the reduction or virtual elimination of commuting time and
the consequent availability of more leisure time. Also,
the general transportation networks in the netropolitan
area would be relieved of some of their rush-hour burden.
Proper zoning and new planning can move us in this direction.

Zoning Is Prohibitive

Zoning has another weakness--its typically prohibitive
nature. The whole character of zoning as we know it today
is highly negative in flavor; the primary purpose of zoning
is to exclude certain land uses.[10] The average zoning ordinance is written so that changes that are dictated by technological progress or other advances cannot be made.

A zoning ordinance may, for instance, prohibit certain
kinds of manufacturing establishments that were considered

nuisances at the time the ordinance was prepared--the exclusion of glue and fertilizer manufacturing is illustrative. But what if technological developments now mean that
glue and fertilizer can be manufactured in perfectly clean
outlets, with no adverse effects on the environment or the
aesthetics of the community? In general, zoning should be
more positive in tone, more sensitive to broad standards
of community development and less to specific uses and prohibitions.

Zoning Weakens the Tax Base

Since there are often too many variables involved, it
is difficult to make categorical statements about the effects of zoning policy on the tax base. The only way that
it is possible to learn the fiscal or tax consequences of
this or that zoning policy is to study the effects of zoning policy in specific communities where all of the relevant factors can be readily observed. Short of this, generalizations are naturally possible although somewhat risky.
Still, this does not preclude the fact that zoning may and
does commonly weaken the tax base.
As noted, one of the more typical reasons given for
exclusionary or fiscal zoning is the tax argument. Expensive housing, it is held, is better for the tax base.
First of all, it should be pointed out that one is not talking about the tax implications of development as opposed
to the implications of no development, as appears to be so
commonly assumed. Also, added costs of public improvements
and services often are confused with tax increases. It is
true that when development is permitted in an area where
there was previously no development, costs of public services
go up; there is no way around this, considering public services in the aggregate. If you add one house, for example,
and that house contains, say, two children of school age, it
is going to cost the county, municipality, or school district so many dollars per year to educate these children.
On the other hand, if that land remains vacant, or is used
for farming or forestry, there will not be this cost. But
this is not the end of the argument, for the owner of the
new house is not simply an economic liability in the community's eyes--the owner also pays taxes on his property, and
perhaps other local taxes. The question is whether the new
citizen pays more in taxes than he receives in services;
in fact, the new resident could become an economic asset to
the community. Outright opposition to new development does

not necessarily make sense from a tax standpoint, yet such reasoning is frequently used.

An important consideration is the type of development put on the presently unused land. Here the issue is whether one pattern of development or land use will be more economically advantageous or less economically disadvantageous to the community than another. That is, will single-family zoning or large-lot zoning net the community more (taxes produced, less costs of public services) or cost the community less (costs of services, less taxes contributed) than multiple-family, commercial, or industrial zoning? In determining the answer to this question, one should consider ideally only those costs and taxes involved in a specific zoning category and the resulting devlopment patterns, a difficult research task indeed.

In the main, it would appear that industrial, commercial, and apartment uses are most attractive from a property tax point of view. These land uses normally can be expected to contribute more in property tax revenues than they cost the community in services. Single-family residential development, on the other hand, does not necessarily fare as well.

Concerning only local school costs and revenues, one study found that high-density residential (apartment), commercial, industrial, and luxury housing uses produced fiscal surpluses (school taxes paid exceeded school costs generated).[11] Most categories of single-family residential development produced fiscal deficits (school costs generated exceeded school taxes paid). In general, whether single-family homes produced surpluses or deficits depended on the number of bedrooms. Usually, units with less than three bedrooms produced surpluses, while those with three or more produced deficits; it was found that homes with a larger number of bedrooms had more students enrolled in the public schools. Also, the school cost-revenue effect of single-family homes was dependent on the price of the unit, with the higher-priced homes ($90,000 range) producing surpluses and middle- and lower-priced units producing deficits.

This same study showed that both production and research industries produced fiscal surpluses, considering school costs generated and school taxes paid. Shopping centers in four different size categories produced over twice as much in school taxes as they generated in school costs. Apartment units with no bedrooms, or with one or two bedrooms, produced surpluses; those with three bedrooms a deficit.

The authors of the study concluded that the land uses that can be expected to be most effective in maintaining balanced growth are, in order of their effectiveness: (1) industrial development; (2) commercial development; (3) luxury homes; and (4) apartments. According to the authors, each of these four land uses "can be expected to offset the cost-revenue deficits of medium-priced single-family homes."

Our concern is not only with actual development or land use but also with the kind of zoning that produces them. If the results of the above study can be taken as typical, it would appear that exclusionary zoning may be fiscally productive if the zoning results in quite high-priced housing (of course, the calculation of all local costs and revenues could alter this picture somewhat). The main question appears to be whether large-lot zoning pro-duces these higher-priced homes. Suburbanites who back large-lot zoning apparently claim that it does. Simple observation does not provide a clear answer to this ques-tion, although it seems as though the typical suburban reasoning is generally correct. But research on the matter suggests a less conclusive answer. One study, conducted at the University of Pennsylvania, discovered that the cor-relation between the lot size and the selling price of homes was low. (This study also found that attitudes toward large lots in the suburbs correlated positively with social rank--i.e., the higher the social rank, the more favorable the attitude toward large-lot development.)[12]

In any event, single-family zoning is by no means clearly a local revenue producer, and certain types of single-family zoning (resulting in middle- and lower-priced housing and units with large numbers of bedrooms) are apt to add, on balance, to a community's tax burden.[13] As noted before, most zoning is for single-family residences, and this includes zoning for middle- and lower-priced housing (in the context of the above study, "middle-priced" housing is that in the $60,000 range, "lower-priced" housing in the $35,000 range). The common practice of zoning out apartments and commercial and industrial development may well be harmful to the community's tax picture. Current suburban zoning trends cannot normally be supported by tax arguments.

Taking a broader view, the costs of servicing a single-family home can run as high as $17,000 a year, according to one assessment; and, although this will come as a shock to some suburbanites, costs can be cut to around $6,000 to $9,000 for certain multifamily developments.[14] These statistics represent only public expenditures, or outlays of all levels of government, and do not reflect the added private spending generated by single-family zoning. Concerning private spending, single-family zoning, extended over a wide area, may mean the absence of neighborhood shopping facilities and require lengthy and expensive drives to such facilities--this is especially true in large-lot zoned areas. The lack of commercial services and facilities and certain other nonresidential land uses in single-family areas may have a similar effect on private spending and may cause great inconvenience and many problems. Residential neighborhoods may have no gas stations and no plumbing, electrical, or other maintenance outlets; even when one or two of these services are available in the area, the absence of competition has a further upward push on service costs. A neighborhood or area may be incomplete because zoning has made key community or public facilities unavailable.

We do not mean to imply that all single-family or large-lot residential zoning is undesirable--on tax grounds or other grounds. In fact, at least some types of development governed by large-lot zoning can properly be defended on tax grounds. There is room in the typical metropolitan area for some purely single-family residential zoning, as there is for some large-lot zoning. There will be many neighborhoods made up exclusively of single-family residences whether we like it or not, for the land area that has been zoned this way typically has been extensively developed. Limited areas of large-lot zoning are appropriate where large-lot development serves a metropolitanwide end--such as working as a buffer between areas of concentrated development--and where other close-in land is available for pressing urban needs.

What cannot be supported is the practice whereby numerous suburban jurisdictions zone much or most of their land into the large-lot categories. The result is that the central city and inner suburbs are surrounded, almost choked, by extensive areas of large-lot development or by large-lot zoning for areas not yet developed; this makes outward migration and growth essentially impossible, not to mention the spiraling effects it has on inner-city and close-in suburban land prices (and consequently on rents and housing and business costs). This sort of zoning and development cannot be justified on any grounds.

TECHNIQUES OF CHANGE

There are a number of specific techniques that can be used to implement the suggestions in this chapter. They include:

1. Cluster zoning, which permits some concentration of development and the conservation of open spaces for common use;
2. Planned unit-development zoning, which encourages variety in land use and provides freedom in planning;
3. New town zoning, which is planned unit-development zoning on a broader scale and which can be used for areas with significant population concentrations;
4. Contract or conditional zoning, which introduces more flexibility into the community development process;
5. Vertical zoning, which provides for different uses within the same structure or building;
6. Site-plan approval, which encourages innovation and mixture in physical development and layout design.

Each of these approaches represents an improvement over the customary stipulations, prohibitions, and limitations of conventional zoning and subdivision control practices, and each is discussed in Chapter 6.

LOCAL AND FEDERAL ACTION
ARE NEEDED

Communities should be encouraged to make the needed adjustments in attitudes and values that will lead to a more progressive zoning policy. Certainly, the primary responsibility for making the necessary changes in policy rests with local authorities. Ultimately, though, federal officials will have to face up to the fact that communities cannot go it alone in zoning. The national government has a right to seek a reform in community zoning practices, considering the amount of federal money pumped into communities. It is the duty of the national government to see to it that federal funds are spent to advance the general interest of the community and the public good in the metropolitan area. Federal money should not be used to prop up discriminatory and exclusionary zoning and subdivision control policies;

it should not be used to underwrite land-use policies that
prevent needed development designed to serve all segments
of the population and that bar needed public, community,
and commercial facilities and services.

NOTES

1. See Richard F. Babcock, The Zoning Game (Madison:
The University of Wisconsin Press, 1966). Babcock puts it
as follows: "Zoning has provided the device for protecting
the homogenous, single-family suburb from the city" (p. 3).
2. For a discussion of the outlooks of the different
classes, see Edward C. Banfield, The Unheavenly City (Boston: Little, Brown, 1970), chap. 3.
3. In 1967, about 43 percent of the total general
revenues of local government came from the property tax;
other local government revenues were derived from state
aid, federal aid, sales taxes, income taxes, other taxes,
and charges. For a discussion of the property tax as a
revenue source in urban governments, see Carl A. McCandless,
Urban Government and Politics (New York: McGraw-Hill,
1970), pp. 361-68. For a tabular presentation of the distribution of local government revenues by source, see Thomas
R. Dye, Politics in States and Communities (Englewood
Cliffs, N.J.: Prentice-Hall, 1969), p. 448.
4. Planning Measures and Controls in Southeastern
Pennsylvania, Pt. 3, Zoning, Fels Institute of Local and
State Government (Philadelphia: University of Pennsylvania,
1960), pp. IV-39, IV-41.
5. For information on fiscal zoning and the data presented above, see Building the American City, National Commission on Urban Problems (Washington, D.C.: Government
Printing Office, 1968), pp. 212-15. The commission found
large-lot zoning to be a "common and widespread practice
in many major metropolitan areas" (p. 214). The commission
conducted extensive research into zoning and other land-
use control and building regulation activities throughout
the nation; it contributed significantly to the literature
in this area.
6. Probably the best study of suburban politics, although somewhat dated, is: Robert C. Wood, Suburbia: Its
People and Their Politics (Boston: Houghton Mifflin, 1958).
For insights into the social structure of the suburbs, see
William M. Dobriner, Class in Suburbia (Englewood Cliffs,
N.J.: Prentice-Hall, 1963). Both Wood and Dobriner consider
reasons for the suburban migration.

7. Brown v. Board of Education of Topeka, Kansas, 347 U.S. 483 (1954).

8. Environmental Quality, The Second Annual Report of the Council on Environmental Quality (Washington, D.C.: Government Printing Office, 1971), p. 213.

9. The disadvantages of rule in small areas are examined in Roscoe C. Martin, Grass Roots (University, Ala.: University of Alabama Press, 1957).

10. As Richard F. Babcock notes, from 1920 to 1940, zoning was "cumulative." "Higher" uses were permitted in "lower" categories, with single-family residential being the "highest," followed by, say, multiple-family residential, commercial, and industrial--in that order. Thus, single-family residences were permitted in any category, and all uses permitted in the industrial zone. After World War II, the principle that each category (district, zone) was to be reserved exclusively for the stipulated use became more common. From the beginning, the integrity of the single-family zone was preserved. Babcock, The Zoning Game, pp. 127-28.

11. This study was conducted in the Barrington, Illinois, area, at the fringe of the Chicago metropolitan area; the area included several local governments, including school districts. Darwin G. Stuart and Robert B. Teska, "Who Pays for What: A Cost-Revenue Analysis of Suburban Land Use Alternatives," Urban Land, XXX, 3 (March 1971), 3-16. Although the study is restricted to school expenditures and revenues, school spending frequently accounts for two-thirds to four-fifths of all local government expenditures in the suburbs; in the Barrington area, it accounted for 72 percent of all local outlays.

12. James G. Coke and Charles S. Liebman, "Political Values and Population Density Control," Land Economics, No. 37 (1961), 354, 357-61.

13. Cf. Ruth L. Mace and Warren J. Wicker, Do Single-Family Homes Pay Their Way? A Comparative Analysis of Costs and Revenues for Public Services, Research Monograph 15 (Washington, D.C.: Urban Land Institute, 1968). The authors of this study suggest that their findings serve to challenge the assumption that "moderately priced, single-family homes . . . do not add to local revenues as much as they add to local costs" (p. 7).

14. Dwight F. Rettie, in a speech at a conference on the future of the Potomac piedmont region, sponsored by the Central Atlantic Environment Service and held in Warrenton, Va., April 1971; reported in the Washington Post, April 25, 1971.

4

THE HOUSING CRISIS

PLANNING AND HOUSING

How are planning and zoning policies and practices related to housing? Let us look at the housing policy area itself and some of the attempts by the three levels of government to deal with housing conditions and the housing problem. We are concerned particularly with the effects of public policy in different fields on housing, the availability of housing generally, the cost of housing, and the supply of housing for low- and moderate-income families.

It is no secret that we Americans have not been able to come to grips with many of the negative aspects of housing, that we have not been able to contain the various forces that are pushing housing costs continuously upward, that we have not been able to eliminate slums, and that we have made only limited progress at best in guaranteeing equal housing opportunities to minorities. In this chapter we shall try to find the way out of the somewhat desperate straits into which we seem to have thrust ourselves in housing and indicate some of the realistic ways in which we can attain our lofty housing objectives.

So far, much of our discussion has centered around the suburbs of the great metropolitan areas of the nation, for this is where planning and zoning have the most meaning, and it is where land-use policy has attracted the greatest attention. In certain respects, however, the housing problem can be viewed as being essentially that of the central city. This is not to suggest by any means that bad housing is limited to the city (the statistics do not indicate this), but it is to say that the most visible deterioration of housing, the greatest concentrations of poor housing,

and, in general, the least desirable housing of the metropolitan region seem to be in the cities.

In the purely quantitative sense, there is likely to
be more unsound and poorly maintained housing in the city
than the suburbs, at least in the major metropolitan areas
of the country. Still, the housing problem in the cities
is not unrelated to actions taken in the suburbs. Housing
conditions in the city, housing costs in the city, the extent of the availability of decent housing for city residents, and rent levels in the city are affected in no un-
certain terms by activity in the suburbs, particularly by
the zoning policy of suburban governments. In this respect,
we still are concerned with the suburbs in this chapter.

It hardly is possible to overestimate the effects that
suburban government policy in land use and building regulation has on housing throughout the typical metropolitan
area. Of course other factors affect city housing conditions since other forces have an important influence on the
housing market, the housing construction costs, and the
housing supply. For instance, inflation may well put housing out of the reach of certain groups by moving housing
costs upward, and the bargaining power of labor as an input
into housing costs should not be discounted. But the direct
action of local government must be a key influence in setting the tone of housing policy and in determining the degree and kind of activity to be found in housing. For
various reasons, government action has the greatest meaning
and the most far-reaching impact in the suburbs, as evi-
denced in planning, zoning, subdivision control, and building code policies. Before getting into this matter though,
let us examine some general figures on housing across the
country.

HOUSING CONDITIONS IN AMERICA

In 1969 some 20 million American citizens lived in
housing units that were below the minimum standards required
for human habitation. Since 1960, the United States had 11
million substandard or overcrowded housing units, and this
constituted 16 percent of the total housing inventory of
the nation. The metropolitan areas alone have some 4
million units of unsound and overcrowded housing, along
with millions of additional dwellings that are deteriorating
and are in violation of local codes and ordinances.

Surprising as it may seem, there is actually propor-
tionately more substandard housing in the suburbs than in

the central cities when all of the over 200 metropolitan areas in the country are considered. Specifically, 16 percent of the owner-occupied dwelling units in the suburbs were found to be unsound,* compared to 11 percent in the central city; 36 percent of the renter-occupied dwelling units in the suburbs were unsound, compared to 33 percent in the central city.[1] By way of explanation, it should be noted that many of us are familiar with housing conditions in the largest of the nation's metropolitan regions but not with conditions in the smaller ones, that socioeconomic differences within the metropolitan areas of certain parts of the South and West do not follow the Eastern and North Central pattern of wealth in the suburbs and poverty in the city, and that the term "suburb" as defined for statistical purposes is not the same as the typical conception that most of us have of the suburbs.

The housing problem for nonwhites is much more marked than it is for whites (considered as a single group). For example, of all renter-occupied housing units in the metropolitan areas, about 35 percent were considered unsound; but this figure rises to between 56 and 70 percent for nonwhites, depending on the portion of the metropolitan area involved. In the owner-occupied category, the percentage of unsound housing units occupied by nonwhites ranges from 33 to 50 percent.

NATIONAL HOUSING GOALS

In 1968 the U.S. Congress set a ten-year housing goal for the nation at 26 million units, or 2.6 million units a year. The total figure is to include 6 million dwellings for low- and moderate-income families, the group that government and private industry have had the hardest time reaching. On the basis of past performance, it is not clear that we can come close to achieving this goal. In the decade 1959-68, the building industry produced at an average annual rate of about 1.5 million units, far below the 2.6 million yearly figure set as a target.[2]

Although the picture presently looks bright, the actual statistics for 1969 showed that housing started to dip slightly below the average for the preceding ten years; in 1970 about 1.4 million units were started, again below the

---

*Unsound housing is that which lacks some or all plumbing facilities, is deteriorating, or is dilapidated.

previous 1.5 million average. (These figures do not include mobile home units; in September 1971, mobile home shipments were running at an annual rate of over 500,000, according to the U.S. Department of Commerce.) While the number of housing units started in 1971 and 1972 were up, the country still is not making sufficient progress toward meeting its housing objectives, even assuming that a higher output would mean we could reach those in the lower-income brackets who are in greatest need, a somewhat dubious assumption.

RESPONSIBILITY FOR HOUSING POLICY

The task of providing housing to the American people is divided among the different governments and private industry. Housing policy is made by the national, state, and local governments. Government at all levels takes action that can affect housing production and the character of the housing market, while the private home-building industry constructs housing. Nearly all housing in the United States is privately owned, and all of it is built by private enterprise (it may be built for government or with government assistance). The national and particularly local governments have the basic public responsibilities in housing; states have limited but expanding assignments in this area.

National Government

The national government helps shape housing policy through the enactment and administration of housing legislation and other measures that affect housing. Federal policy in housing per se is administered by the U.S. Department of Housing and Urban Development (HUD). In addition, Washington has important monetary powers that can have a significant effect on housing finances and therefore on housing production. A tight monetary policy at the national level can dry up the funds available to the housing industry, and a number of federal actors, especially the Federal Reserve Board and the President, can help mold this policy. National agencies concerned directly with housing, other than HUD, include the Government National Mortgage Association (Ginnie Mae), the Federal National Mortgage Association (Fannie Mae, previously a government unit, but now a private, government-sponsored organization), and the Federal Home Loan Bank Board.

There were particularly notable national housing enact-
ments in 1937 (public housing), 1949 (urban redevelopment),
1954 (urban renewal), and 1961 (special low-income housing
assistance). The national government's housing programs
have been modified and expanded over the years, and most
observers believe that healthy advances have been made
through new legislation in housing. For instance, in 1965
a rent supplement plan was introduced, and in 1968 new
homeownership and rental features were added to housing
measures in yet further attempts to assist low- and moderate-income families.

State Governments

It has been only recently that the state governments
have done much in housing, and their involvement still
remains limited. State government activity in housing and
urban development has been concentrated largely in several
of the key, more industrialized, and highly populated states
like New York, New Jersey, and Massachusetts, although
certain exceptions can be cited.[3] Traditionally, the role
of the states in this field has been restricted to authorizing local government action in such areas as planning,
land-use control, building and housing regulation, public
housing, and urban renewal.

Local Governments

Probably the most important governmental activity in
housing is found at the local level. The communities have
the essential control over housing and the home-building
industry; fundamental power over housing is exercised by
local government. It is at the local level that change
will have to be made if indeed it is going to be made at
all.

Local governments regulate housing and building activity and land use; local regulations significantly affect
the home-building industry and its organization. The home-
building industry is dominated by relatively small builders, numbering over 100,000; these builders are spread
across the United States. The National Association of
Home Builders--the major home contractors' trade group--
alone has over 50,000 members, composed mostly of builders.
The largest of the builders is Levitt and Sons, at the
moment a subsidiary of International Telephone and Telegraph

(Levitt and Sons, Inc., a builder of single-family homes,
is a subsidiary of ITT-Levitt). A wide gap separates
Levitt from the second leading producer of homes. Only 22
home builders do over $20 million of business each year,
and less than 60 do $10 million or over. Sixty-five per-
cent of the builders of single-family homes put up less
than 25 units annually; only slightly over 2 percent build
more than 250 units a year.[4]

At present, housing is built on the site, one house
and one element at a time; a wide array of subcontractors
are responsible for most of the work. Under current construction techniques, home-building costs are quite high;
this has a negative effect on the breadth of the market
that ultimately can be served. So far, the middle- and
upper-income groups have been able to absorb the economic
consequences of high-cost housing and of decentralization
in the home-building industry. But low-income families
often have been left out since they have not been able to
afford the expensive housing produced by this process.
Actually, it is questionable whether even middle- and upper-
income groups could afford such costly housing if it were
not for federal housing and related policies that have in
effect served to underwrite the middle-class housing market. FHA and VA programs are especially significant in
this respect as they have assured decent housing on good
terms to large numbers of middle-economic-range families.
Higher-income persons have benefited from the institution-
alizing effects of federal loan policies in the mortgage
industry and are therefore able to live in housing that is
much more expensive than they might be able to afford without federal influence. (The role of the federal government
is normally that of guaranteeing loans and putting an upper
limit on mortgage interest rates; of course, not all loans
are backed by government, but the terms of those not so
backed, called conventional loans, have certainly been affected by government policies.) One could reasonably argue,
therefore, that quality housing has been brought within the
reach of all classes but those in the low-income categories;
government policy is at least partially responsible for
this.

The current organization of the housing industry
drives costs upward, a pattern not dictated by economic
necessity but essentially by the character of government
land-use and building controls. Naturally, a number of
builders are happy with the present situation, having ad-
justed to the constraints imposed; but many others are not
--they are anxious to grow and expand and want to extend

the beneifts of technological advances to homeowners in the
form of lower housing prices. Further, there are a host
of big companies that are prepared to make substantial investments in the home-building business if large-scale
operations covering wide geographical areas can be sustained. The fact of the matter is that mass production
techniques are available and ready to be put into effect
if government policy would permit their use. Industry is
geared up to the task. Local government regulations and
codes stand in the way.

The public regulation of housing, building, and land
use is largely, almost exclusively, a local responsibility
in the United States. This means that the basic power over
housing is in the hands of numerous, independent governments operating in limited geographical settings with small
populations. To be exact, over 14,000 local governments
in this country have the building regulation authority--
and this includes planning, zoning, subdivision regulation,
building code, housing code, and local building permit
powers. Of some 18,000 local governments that might be
assumed to have such authority, the incidence of land and
building regulatory power is as follows:[5]

	Number of Governments with Activity
Zoning ordinance	9,595
Subdivision regulation	8,086
Building code	8,344
Housing code	4,904
Any of these (including planning board) or a local building permit system	14,088

Public building and land-use regulatory authority is
then a thoroughly decentralized matter, but this in itself
does not tell us much. From the standpoint of the organization of the home-building industry, what is more important
is the substantive nature of the regulations over construction and land use from community to community. In fact,
the various housing, land-use, and building codes and ordinances are not uniform; they are often restrictive and often impose high construction costs on builders. Because
of these regulations, techniques of standardization, industrialized construction, and assembly-line processes cannot
be used in residential construction.

As an example, a builder in the metropolitan area of Cleveland must cope with 50 different codes controlling building activity. Home contractors in greater Chicago must comply with the same number of independent building regulatory controls; 30 distinct building codes stand firmly in the way of more economical construction in the Minneapolis region. To make matters worse, most local governments do not have building codes that conform to one of the generally accepted national models. To illustrate, many localities prohibit the use of plastic pipes in housing as well as preassembled electrical wiring and plumbing systems, all of which represent advances toward economical construction and which have been proved scientifically to be sound and effective.

Zoning can have a major impact on building and housing costs and construction practices. Zoning controls the specific use of land, lot size, setbacks, and population densities, and as such it has more influence on land development than any of the other regulatory measures. Like building codes, zoning works to fragment the housing and building industry. Because of the decentralized character of zoning administration, because of the uneven application of zoning controls even within a single community, and because of the rigidity of most zoning ordinances, this government power typically discourages all but small-scale building endeavors. Further, zoning restrictions on population density (requiring low densities) and lot size (requiring high minimums) make major housing undertakings impractical in large segments of the urban and metropolitan region.

All evidence points to the conclusion that local government regulatory controls directly or indirectly account for the conditions in and the organization of the home-building industry; they are therefore a principal cause of high-cost housing.[6] However, the existing policies of local government would not have survived without the support of influential forces in communities, and such policies obviously serve the interests of key local groups who have for one reason or another become dependent on them. A change in these policies is not likely without significant pressure from the outside.

Local governments engage in other activities that affect housing. Municipalities and counties, for instance, have the basic administrative control over public housing and urban renewal in our system of government, although general policy guidelines and much of the money come from Washington. It is in this sense that community public housing and urban renewal efforts are to be distinguished

from community land-use and building-housing regulation
powers, as the latter are virtually exclusively local responsibilities (perhaps influenced by national officials an
and public policy). Well over 1,500 public housing authorities are found at the local level throughout the country,
normally operating with a certain degree of independence
of general-purpose local governments (public housing units
are usually counted as special districts by the U.S. Bureau
of the Census). Up to 1968, such agencies had constructed
close to 700,000 housing units for low-income residents,
according to the National Commission on Urban Problems;
as noted, the public housing program was initiated under
federal legislation enacted in 1937.

Many localities also have urban renewal and redevelopment authorities or agencies that plan and carry out face-
lifting and rebuilding activities in core (and other) areas.
Although urban renewal legislation and directions have been
modified somewhat of late, urban renewal has had a largely
negative impact on the supply of housing for low-income
residents, tending thereby to counterbalance the effects
of public housing policy. Still, urban renewal has had
other more favorable consequences, including changing the
image of some central cities, eliminating run-down housing,
securing central city investments, improving the prospects
of attracting new capital to cities, and inducing middle-
income residents to move back into core areas.

Politics of Community Policies
Affecting Housing

To provide better insight into the roots of community
policies affecting housing, we briefly will discuss the
politics of these policies--including land-use controls,
urban renewal, public housing, and building codes. We do
not cover housing codes (they are part of the local housing
regulatory powers) because they do not have as much of an
effect on housing costs or the housing supply as the other
powers or programs. (Of the relevant regulatory powers,
building codes govern construction, land-use controls concern land, and housing codes deal with maintenance-occupancy
and owner-supplied facilities standards; the building and
land-use powers have the greatest bearing on housing costs
and supply.)

In considering housing policies, local politics should
not be confused with national politics, and politics should
not be equated with Republican or Democratic partisanship
in communities.

It is common to think of the Democratic party as the
more liberal of the two national parties. The best test
of liberalism is action in specific policy areas; by this
test, in housing, the Democratic party stands up well.
It was the Democratic party that sponsored the housing
legislation of the 1930s; on the public housing bill backed
by the Roosevelt administration and passed in 1937, the
House GOP was united in opposition (with one defection),
the Senate Republicans were fairly evenly split, but the
Democrats in both bodies overwhelmingly supported the bill.
In more recent times, in 1965, presidential and congres-
sional Democrats favored the rent supplement plan, while
Republicans in both chambers of Congress were generally opposed. Over the years, the GOP has been more favorable to
the private enterprise than to the social welfare features
of the various housing bills; the Democrats have favored
both features.

The liberal-conservative split evident at the national
level does not necessarily carry over to the local level,
at least so far as housing matters are concerned. Locally,
there are important divisions over housing and land-use
policy, but these divisions seldom follow strict party lines.
The explanation of this is somewhat complex, but there are
identifiable reasons. First, both parties at the local
level are essentially independent of their national units;
as noted in Chapter 1, the typical view is that power in
both parties flows from the bottom up rather than from the
top down. In any event, considerable independence is found
in the local parties. With this independence, local parties
have a certain freedom of action that allows them to veer
from national stands or to develop their own policy positions. Thus, a local Democratic party may be more conservative than its generally liberal national wing, and community Republicans may be to the left of the generally conservative national GOP.

Second, the specific issues in the housing area vary
from the national to the local level and, further, may involve different uses of government powers. At the local
level, for example, land-use controls are a key housing
issue. Such an issue is difficult to discuss in conservative or liberal terms, and conservative and liberal stands
are hard to identify. While we may be in agreement on
what the conservative position is on national housing legislation, what can we identify as a conservative stand on
zoning? In addition, local housing issues may involve different uses of government powers than national housing issues. This may cause the same people to view housing matters differently at different levels. As an example, a

liberal Democrat at the national level may support rent
subsidies to the poor, and at the same time be wary of the
use of zoning at the local level; rent subsidies have limited effects on the private enterprise system (they may,
in fact, serve to strengthen it in important ways), while
the zoning power may affect significantly the economic
system and especially an individual's right to use his
economic resources (land, buildings) as he pleases. In
this sense, a national liberal Democrat may be a conservative Democrat at the community level.

By the same token, the Republican party at the local
level is not necessarily the "business party" that it tends
to be in national councils. In fact, in any number of
middle- to upper-income Republican suburbs, housing and
land-use controls, often shaped by the local GOP, are distinctly antibusiness. Such controls may be designed to
keep out unwanted classes of residents or to protect property values, but in any event they are apt to have a negative effect on the local business community. In this respect, a national conservative Republican may oppose rent
subsidies as an unwarranted use of government power but he
may strongly back zoning as a desirable use of government
power. Economic interests, of course, may dictate such an
apparently inconsistent stand, as they might in our Democratic example above. Business is not the only force in
society that has economic interests to protect in politics.

It should be noted that much action of local government in regulating housing and land use can work against
private business; such action would include the adoption
of burdensome controls, overly restrictive regulations, and
policies that unnecessarily delay the execution of land
development proposals. Most developers accept the principle
that government has every right to control land use and
building practices but they oppose legislative and administrative action that places needless obstacles in the path
of development--needless, that is, in terms of the promotion of the general health, welfare, and safety of the community. It is the upper-middle-income suburbs, nearly always dominated by Republican voters and often by local GOP
public officeholders, that are most apt to impose requirements on business that go beyond the goal of protecting
the public interest. The same principle holds even if local
elections are nonpartisan or if the Democratic party controls the community policy-making apparatus. Nonpartisan
rule often means, in effect, Republican rule,[7] and local
Democrats are likely to see things the same way the local
GOP does, for both are appealing to the same small set of

voters--single-family homeowners. In some communities,
though, developers have found Democrats more willing to
make concessions than Republicans, possibly because of the
latter's solid and almost exclusive base in upper-income
residential neighborhoods; it is such neighborhoods that
frequently favor local land-use policy that clamps rigid
controls on developers.

Particular pressures often account for the nature of
community land-use and building regulation policies. These
pressures may have little or nothing to do with national
party or political patterns and ideological conflicts.
Still, one cannot help pointing out a certain degree of inconsistency in suburban Republicans who vote conservatively
in national elections, who exert a conservative influence
on the national Republican party, and who are unapologeti-
cally probusiness in political philosophy. What happens
to these Republicans when it comes to local government policy in land-use and building regulation? What has happened
to the conservative doctrine? How can they oppose government interference with business in Washington but strongly
support it in the community? The answer, of course, is not
to be found in any set of abstract principles but, as suggested, in these Republicans' perception of their own interests.

No matter how one may explain this inconsistency in
theoretical terms, practically speaking the suburbanite is
likely to find a sort of business-oriented conservatism to
be most compatible with his economic interests at the national level, while he is likely to warm up to the antibusiness forces (which he will picture otherwise) in the
community since he feels that such a stance will best protect his economic interests (property values) at the local
level. While the government may be seen as a disruptive
force at the national level, threatening one's economic
status, it is business that is the villain in the community.
For developers and builders may change land-use patterns;
they may introduce commercial uses into a residential
neighborhood, they may construct high-rise apartments,
and, most important, they may build housing for groups of
lower economic status, of different races, or of minority
ethnic or religious affiliation.

In two respects, the suburban Republican is really
quite consistent: first, he consistently favors his own
interests--in this case mostly economic--and this causes
him to oppose government control at the national level and
to back it locally; second, he lines up on the side of the
status quo at both levels, indiscriminately working against

change in both places, whether this change is initiated by government (national) or business (local). Change is the real threat, and it may be opposed on both ideological and economic grounds. Instructively, the conflict evident among suburban Republicans is not found among most liberal Democrats, who favor restrictions on business at all levels.

The second point made at the beginning of this section was that politics is not the same as partisanship. The reason for this has already been suggested to some extent. As pointed out in Chapter 1, a number of forces in addition to political parties are apt to be involved in setting community land-use and housing policy, and, more often than not, the parties respond to the wishes of such forces. In the suburbs, this frequently means that the parties are particularly sensitive to the interests of neighborhood citizens groups, composed of residential neighborhood home-owners. Parties also may seek to take into account the views of the real estate community, although the role of developers in suburban land-use policy seems to be de-clining.

It is in this sense that the base of housing and land-use politics in the community may be found outside the frame-work of the two parties. The two parties tend to play the role of representing the fundamental interests of the commu-nity, at least so far as housing and land-use policy is concerned. Both parties will attempt to represent as many interests as are needed to assure victory at the polls, and in the suburbs, the homeowners' interest is commonly the key one. In this light, it is unlikely that one party will be clearly or exclusively linked with the developers' point of view while the other is linked with that of the citizens groups. Both parties will try to identify with the latter, and this is likely to have implications for political and public policy. However, either or both of the parties may be dependent on developer funds, and this also could affect public decisions.

In our political system, pressures from particular interests are more apt to explain public policy than ab-stract philosophical principles. Where pressures are not openly or directly exerted, they still are likely to be evident, as policy-makers, especially elected officials, tend to prefer to please important interests. Many, per-haps most, public officials have values that can be readily identified and are apt to act in accordance with these values without being pressured. Naturally, interest groups such as citizens or developers associations consider the values of candidates for appointed or elected office before extending their support. In a more practical sense, citizens groups will back officials who think the way they do; in the land-use, housing, and building regulation areas, this means that these groups will support officials who oppose changing the residential character of the suburbs, who are happy with single-family development patterns, who favor strong restrictions on developers, who are wary of commercial uses, and who oppose high-density residential development. All of these points and others can be wrapped up in a philosophy that can be detected in short order by citizens association leaders.

A somewhat specialized type of politics seems to exist in the area of building code policy. This is a matter than seldom if ever has been researched systematically, and thus little scientific data on it can be cited. It would appear that building code officials are themselves a considerable political force in their area of interest and can mold the substance of building codes and the character of the administrative practices associated with these codes. Building code officials are organized at the national (or regional) level through different groups, and the national organizations of building code officials develop model codes and standards that have much influence over the provisions in building codes at the local level. Some experts have noted, as did the Douglas Commission, that communities do not follow all provisions in model codes; this does not mean that model codes are not influential or do not serve as guides in the community. Another force that typically has an interest in the content of local building codes is labor unions, namely the building and construction trades. Builders and suppliers also are likely to have a voice in the community building code process.[8]

The politics of urban renewal and public housing deserves special mention. Both urban renewal and public housing are examples of cooperative national-local government programs, and much policy in both areas is made at the local level. In the past, major downtown business interests commonly have had a significant effect on the direction of urban renewal policy; these interests have included big department stores, the larger banks, and community developers. It was such interests that provided the key backing for the national urban renewal legislation initially passed by the federal government in the late 1940s (the program was enacted in 1949, but the term urban renewal was not used until 1954).

A good example of how urban renewal works can be cited in Philadelphia, where policies and priorities often were determined by the business-dominated Greater Philadelphia Movement (GPM) and its allies in municipal government, political, and intellectual circles. This was the coalition that hoisted Democratic bluebloods Joseph Clark and Richardson Dilworth to power, crushed the ruling Republican machine, and launched an ambitious urban renewal program in the central core of the city. At present, the interests of minority racial groups have a much greater influence over urban renewal decision-making than they have had in the past.[9]

The public housing program in communities appears to have been under the control of New Deal-oriented liberals, not businessmen, at least for the years following the program's initiation in the 1930s. Of course, the public housing effort has not had the wide-ranging impact on downtown redevelopment and the community's general image that urban renewal has had; this may help explain the absence of substantial business representation on local public housing authorities. As with urban renewal, the federal funding and independent local administration of public housing (through a separate authority) have permitted public housing supporters to work somewhat outside the community power structure and have served to give them added leverage inside this power structure. In recent years, public housing project residents have been organized through tenant councils, and these councils represent tenants in the public housing political and decision-making process; for years, tenant organizations were banned in some cities.

EFFECTS OF HOUSING POLICIES

The effect of land-use and building regulation policies at the community level has been clear: high-cost construction and high-priced housing. In a sense, we might be able to give local authorities a higher score in this regard if we consider the point that local land development and building regulations are directed only in part at housing (they may serve planning and other ends in addition to providing decent housing to the residents).

Some housing policies, however, are aimed specifically at housing. Public housing is an example. In public housing, the production rate has not come close to meeting the need; thousands remain on the waiting lists for public housing in different cities and countries throughout the nation. One often hears the argument that if only the government would step up its commitment to public housing in the community we could go a long way toward overcoming the housing problem. We are told that what is needed is more money. This line of reasoning has to be questioned. Although more public housing assistance is needed and is currently being provided (public housing starts in the early 1970s are up over the levels of the 1960s), it is not certain that the pace of housing starts could be appreciably increased under almost any circumstances.

The reason for this assessment lies in neighborhood resistance to housing for low-income persons, including public housing. This resistance commonly finds its way into city and county governing bodies where it is translated into public policy.[10] This problem will not likely subside as public housing officials seek to disperse public housing throughout the community and to integrate it with middle-income housing, although the problem may get worse. In any event, local objections to particular sites for public housing pose at least as much of an obstacle as a lack of funds or the absence of sufficient government commitment.

Although public housing authorities are usually technically independent of the local general-purpose city or county government, this independence by no means assures freedom to determine the location of public housing. The city or county government may influence or dictate decisions about the location of public housing sites by putting pressure on the housing authority to reverse location decisions (the housing authority board is typically appointed by the chief executive and/or governing body of the general-purpose government); by withholding needed zoning for public housing (the location of public housing may require a zoning change, which is a general-purpose government responsibility); or by refusing to approve the acquisition of the land for public housing. Middle-income neighborhood interests, opposed to the proposed location of public housing in their area, not uncommonly press city and county officials to veto housing authority decisions on particular sites. Community resistance to housing for the poor has reached staggering proportions.

The urban renewal program has several objectives. One is to provide housing to those who need it (this is an objective of the national legislation, which includes the urban renewal program).* Urban renewal in the main has not

---

*This was an important point of controversy several years ago when urban renewal was held to have cut into the supply of low-income housing. The question was then raised as to the program's objectives.

helped the cause of low-income housing and usually has worked to decrease the supply of housing for the poor and increase it for middle-income groups. Although housing for low- and moderate-income groups, including public housing, is now more commonly a part of the urban renewal effort, the old record, negative in this respect, still stands. Urban renewal typically has razed the residences of the poor and replaced them with housing that can be afforded only by the wealthy or middle-economic-range families. So marked was this tendency that the program became tagged as "Negro removal" by some critics, as the residents who were moved out of urban renewal project areas were frequently black and those subsequently moving in were usually white.

Urban renewal has become the target of some on the right and left, at least in part because of its consequences. One of the sharpest attacks has come from Martin Anderson, author of The Federal Bulldozer.[11] Anderson has called for the program's abolition. While a number of Anderson's criticisms of urban renewal seem to be valid, the program has served many worthy ends and it should be salvaged and revamped, a process well under way at present. The effort simply must be tailored to accord with the objectives of housing legislation, the most important of which is to provide decent homes for all Americans.

Many attempts have been made to extend the benefits of the FHA program and the federal loan guarantee principle to low-income groups. Other efforts are being made to provide better housing for the poor. In 1954 the national housing legislation was amended to make FHA benefits available to the poor under certain conditions. In 1961 what was viewed as a bold new program, the "221-d-3" plan, was introduced. In 1968 key features were added to the housing legislation in yet another attempt to provide housing on reasonable terms to the poor. But in the main these programs have been singularly unsuccessful. They have been unable to overcome the forces that are keeping low- and moderate-income housing from being constructed, and being constructed where it is needed. To a certain extent, the common criticism of the federal bureaucracy, especially of the FHA, is valid, as federal administrative procedures and practices obviously have slowed down whatever progress has been made in this area. But the problem is much deeper than this.

The widely heralded "221-d-3" program has been particularly disappointing; by the late 1960s, it had produced on a nationwide basis only slightly over 50,000 housing

units, mostly for moderate-income families. In the Housing
Act of 1968, loans at as low as 1 percent could in effect
be made to low-income citizens to buy and rent good housing, with the difference between the market interest rate
and 1 percent being made up in the form of a subsidy from
Washington. Although preliminary reports are optimistic,
it is still too early to determine the long-term effects
of the 1968 measure.

The question remains, why have the various housing
policies failed? The answer seems clear: the problem is
in the community. Community regulations and practices make
it hard to construct any kind of low-income housing project.
The existence of the land-use control and development control power in local government has given many residents
the feeling that they have a right to dictate who (in terms
of race, religion, and economic class) will be permitted
to live in their community and the specific kind of housing
he shall have. In a broader sense, the presence of community governments operating according to the principle of
majority rule has given suburban residents the idea that
they have an inherent right to determine what new residents,
if any, will be allowed to move into the community. The
fact of the matter is that if existing residents do not
want a certain economic or racial group living in their
neighborhood, they are encouraged by land-use and development controls to exclude them. The way these controls
have been used in the recent past has been responsible for
this.

In view of present land and development controls and
their use, it is clear that not all the money in the world
will build low-income housing in many suburbs. The federal
government can pour additional billions into its different
housing programs, but it is doubtful whether this would
have much effect in the suburbs. As suggested, it is in the
suburbs that low- and moderate-income housing is so greatly
needed, and it is the suburbs that typically contain the
vacant and nonurbanized land that could be used for new
housing.

As long as communities resist low- and moderate-income
residents, all the new legislation Washington could conceiv-
ably pass will not be likely to achieve the desired objective. This is why new legislation is not apt to succeed
where present laws have failed. Basically, the peg will
not fit into the hole--that is, the federal peg will not
fit into the community hole. The most expensive and refined
peg will not do the job if it does not fit, and so far it
has not.

Much federal housing policy has been based on the premise that there will be no fundamental change in land-use
controls and building codes. The idea has been to funnel
additional dollars and programs into the community to
"cover" the high building costs in a quest to house the
poor. Generally, federal policy has been to avoid taking
on high-cost building practices directly, although the
Operation Breakthrough program of the federal Department of
Housing and Urban Development was beginning to deal with
this matter. Yet the success of normal federal policy requires community acceptance of low- and moderate-income
housing; without this acceptance, the policy will not work.
It is not likely that community attitudes toward housing
the poor will change in the near future, but community development regulations can be changed. With a change in
these regulations, federal housing policy can work.

Community opposition to low- and moderate-income housing is commonly manifest in zoning calling for single-family
residential development only--especially zoning of the more
exclusionary variety. Developers wishing to construct
lower-income housing projects have to apply for a rezoning
under such circumstances; this gives localities an effective
veto. Privately built lower-income housing, unlike public
housing, does not have to receive the government's bless-
ing per se, but, being private, it must be placed on appro-
priately zoned land. Zoning then becomes the base of the
community's power to exclude housing for those less advan-
taged than the existing residents.

Local governments cannot, of course, oppose low-income
housing projects because they are for low-income groups--
this would probably be in violation of the federal and state
constitutions and would furthermore project a bad image.
What happens is that communities oppose the projects on
other grounds, at least for the record, finding that the
new housing would place an excessive burden on the schools,
that the street network will not accommodate the additional
traffic, that community facilities are insufficient, that
no public transportation exists to serve the prospective
new residents, and so on. In fact, any reason other than
that the new residents would be poor and perhaps black is
trotted to the fore. In this manner, the localities of the
nation are using land-use controls in an economically and
racially discriminatory fashion. Everyone knows it; no
one, if sufficiently pressed, would argue otherwise.

The irony of this is that so many in the suburbs favor
the idea of housing for low-income groups. "We support it
in principle" is the common ring. Suburban planners, elected

officials, and citizens group leaders publicly proclaim
their desire to serve all economic classes, to provide
housing for all income groups; they heartily endorse the
doctrine of low- and moderate-income (some limit the endorse-
ment to "moderate-income") housing. But what happens when
they are confronted with a specific proposal? The answer
is easy--they oppose it. The explanation may be that the
particular proposal was a bad one, or that it was at the
wrong location or the wrong time.

Why so many in the suburbs insist on supporting low-
income housing in principle and then turn around and oppose
it in practice is not entirely clear. It may have something to do with the image that they wish to foster. In
any event, the situation is not good, for it gives well-
meaning people the impression that there is a chance to
get low-income housing approved when there is not; it often
diverts attention from the real problem until it is too
late. We have to find another alternative.

WHAT ARE THE ALTERNATIVES?

Present policy has not served the nation's housing
needs. What are alternative policies, alternative strategies? Let us look at the possibilities.

State Action

It is proper to start at this level because some experts
put such heavy reliance on the states in advancing solutions
to the housing problem. Some have suggested that states
impose standards on local governments, forcing the latter
to revise land-use control policies and building regulation
practices. It also has been suggested that the states get
directly into the land-use and building control business
if localities do not clean their own houses.

It is hard to disagree with Daniel J. Elazar that the
states are important and vital participants in the American
federal system.[12] Furthermore, the states surely can make
a significant contribution to improving land development
decision-making processes through, for example, the creation
of new courts of ecology (see Chapter 6). But in general
the states are ill-equipped to handle zoning and housing
matters. It would be nice if this were not so; theoretically
and legally local governments and local powers exist at the
sufferance of the state. But the states have not been di-

rectly involved in land-use, housing, and building regulation matters in the past, and, with exceptions, there is no evidence that they have the ability or desire to become so involved now.

Zoning is properly a local responsibility, and no state other than Hawaii and perhaps one or two others has more than the most limited powers in this field. Some states have embarked on important statewide housing programs (New York is an example), but, in the main, the states have done little in this area. It is not only that state governments have not done much in land use and housing but, more important, there is no reason to expect that they will do what the localities are not doing. States do not operate in the abstract; they are subject to the same general constituencies, the same general pressures, and the same general political constraints as local governments. (This was discussed in relation to planning in Chapter 2.) To expect otherwise would be to expect political magic. And what is worse, the states are becoming increasingly subject to pressures from suburbanites, for it is the suburban areas that have been gaining the most in population and that have benefited most from the Supreme Court's "one-man, one-vote" order in state legislatures.[13] It is, of course, in the suburbs that we have run into the most difficulty in building housing for the poor. Why suburban voters would instruct their state delegations to take action that these voters have prohibited their local officials from taking is not at all clear--and this is precisely what would have to occur if the states are to move "decisively" in land use and housing. Why would suburbanites accept low-income housing at the state level while opposing it locally? Why would suburbanites support racially integrated housing if proposed by the state while blocking such housing locally? Middle- and upper-middle-income suburbanites hold the trump card in either case, and there is no reason to suppose that they would not use it.

The record of New York State's Urban Development Corporation is instructive. The New York Urban Development Corporation probably represents the most advanced form of state involvement in community housing matters; the agency has the authority to undertake low- and moderate-income housing, industrial, civic, and land improvement projects. In the fall of 1970, two years after the organization's establishment, it had 17 projects under way. Yet the Urban Development Corporation goes into a community only by invitation. Although it has the power to override local

zoning and building code regulations, it has not done so.[14]
Experience suggests that the Urban Development Corporation
is quite sensitive to both legislative and local pressures
(which may be one and the same).[15]

Federal Action

The federal role in housing and land use should be
twofold: first, the national government should continue
its present programs in public housing, urban renewal,
and private low- and moderate-income housing assistance,
broadening these efforts to serve wider ends; second,
federal authorities should begin prodding local governments
to take the necessary action to assure sites for housing
for all income groups, especially in the suburbs.

The key to federal involvement is found in the second
area, for the achievement of the objectives in the first
category can be significantly inhibited by undesirable
local policies. Ideally, federally assisted low-income
housing, whether public or private, should be scattered
or dispersed throughout communities, a practice consistent
with the most recent emphasis in federal policy. But, to
the extent that this means that low-income housing should
be located in outlying middle-income city and suburban
areas, local policy will have to accommodate such efforts,
not frustrate them as it typically does at present. This
leads to a discussion of community action.

Local Action

What can be done locally? It is the community that
holds the key to housing; it is the community that has the
power to broaden the housing market and to open housing to
low-income families and to others who need it but are unable
to get it in appropriate locations.

Presently, community land-use, housing, and building
regulations are too rigid and restrictive. More flexibility
should be introduced into the community land development
control process. Flexibility would be preferable to making
local codes and regulations uniform from community to community. One can scarcely object in principle to uniform codes
or ordinances, but any particular model legislation should
be examined carefully; uniformity in and of itself assures
little. One might ask why, if uniformity is the goal, it
would not be more appropriate just to enact one development

code for the entire nation, administered by the national government? Model codes and ordinances are, of course, available, mostly from public interest groups.

Laws and policies in zoning, subdivision regulation, and construction practices should be designed in broad fashion, serving to establish general principles and performance standards that apply to whatever method, approach, or development idea proposed. Communities should avoid overly specific and detailed stipulations; they should avoid adopting laws, ordinances, codes, policies, and practices that permit only one layout pattern, only a single building method, only certain building materials, only one development scheme. The present concepts in community land development and building policies too often work against innovation, experimentation, and economical techniques. The current prohibitive and negative land-use and development policies cannot help us provide housing to the income groups that need it. More flexible policies can mean more efficient construction, more efficient layout patterns, and greater variety in housing prices.

Communities also can develop policies that are more directly aimed at the provision of housing for low- and moderate-income families. One proposal that has merit is the use of the zoning ordinance to assure that at least some low- and moderate-income family housing is built. Zoning regulations can be written so as to provide that a certain proportion of the units of new subdivisions be built for needy families. We caution against excessive controls, restrictions, or requirements in this regard, but most developers probably will accept a reasonable ordinance of this variety. It should be remembered that existing zoning, subdivision, and other community regulations have contributed significantly to the shortage of housing, where needed, for low- and moderate-income families; under current regulations, even if developers wanted to, they could not provide housing for such families.

It makes sense that local regulations be written to permit and stimulate developers to serve lower-income groups. There is no reason why the zoning ordinance should not stipulate that 5 to 15 percent of the total housing units in a subdivision be provided for these groups. This figure is high enough to serve a number of families in need, but not so high so as to discourage development altogether. In this regard, some people have gone on record favoring higher percentages and the rigid imposition of such requirements on developers. But it should be noted that all private housing in the United States is financed through private channels, and this is true whether or not the housing is assisted by government programs or is backed by government loan guarantees. The ultimate decision on whether money is going to be made available for housing is made in the private sphere--by banks, savings and loan associations, insurance companies, and others in the lending business. Developers and many others compete for this money. If provisions that are too inflexible or demanding are written into land-use ordinances, lenders simply may refuse to put money in proposed developments governed by these ordinances. Developers who must have such loans to build will therefore be unable to undertake construction, and development will come to an end. That this could happen is not outside the realm of possibility.

Metropolitanwide action on this front would be helpful. It might be useful if metropolitan-areawide agencies would encourage the major local governments of the metropolitan area to adopt somewhat similar zoning provisions for low- and moderate-income family housing. One advantage of this would be that no single community would have to put itself in a competitively disadvantageous position by being the only one in the area to enact such an ordinance. (Of course, some locality will have to start the ball rolling, but others should be urged to follow.) This would, in addition, keep pressure off any given community to enact unreasonably high minimum percentages. It is also true that the need for low- and moderate-income housing is fairly widespread throughout the typical metropolitan area; each community ideally should share in achieving the desired end. It is mostly suburban governments that would be affected by this idea since it is outlying areas that contain the most undeveloped land suitable for new subdivisions.

Local governments also might consider expanding the housing market to new groups by providing incentives to developers and builders. For instance, in return for the building of low- and moderate-income housing, local officials could permit developers increased densities, less restrictive lot-size and setback requirements, the use of the cluster concept in subdivision layout, or a wider variety of land uses than would be otherwise allowed. The principle is that through any one of these variations, developers could likely reduce the per unit costs of such developer-funded facilities as the road network, curbs and gutters, sewer and water lines, and other public improvements. Greater densities, fewer residential restrictions, cluster subdivision, and a wide variety of land uses are apt to mean more efficient and economical operations for the

developer in other respects as well. Developers could
pass these savings on to prospective homebuyers, perhaps
mostly or entirely in the form of reduced-cost housing for
low- and moderate-income families.

Another approach would be for communities to provide
the developer with subsidies. This money would make up
the difference between the market price and what poor families could afford for housing. This would not be an easy
activity to administer, and the legal implications of such
a move would have to be thoroughly examined; but the principle involved would be essentially the same as that which
applies in the federal rent supplement program (and in
other federal housing programs for that matter). Under
this plan, the developer would make a certain portion of
homes in a subdivision available to low-income residents,
and this could be best accomplished on a scattered-site
basis.

The ideal situation is the mixing of different economic groups or levels in the same general neighborhood;
this is suggested not only because it has ethical appeal
but also because it is necessary from a practical point of
view. But short of this, thought should be given to locating high-density housing for low-income families near
commercial facilities. This is proposed in part because
such housing is less likely to be strongly opposed by middle-income residents and because of the resulting short
distance between work and home. Again, this idea has the
greatest applicability in the suburbs where the need for
housing for low-income workers is most marked. The zoning
for the location of housing near businesses and offices
naturally would have to come from the local government.

Another approach would be for local governments to
undertake some of the costs of development of new subdivisions. As noted, developers typically cover the costs of
key land improvements and public facilities. If the local
government were willing to absorb part of these costs, this
obviously would reduce the developer's financial burden
and he could therefore lower the ultimate price of homes.
It is no secret that developers' costs are reflected in
the price of homes. It would be reasonable for the local
government to do this since the improvements and facilities
provided by the developer are for the benefit of the entire
community (roads are a good example). Of course, some
means would have to be found to assure that the economies
realized would be used to advance decent housing to low-
and moderate-income groups; this could be done by ordinance.
This plan, geared to new subdivisions, would likely have a

broader and more far-reaching effect than one in which subsidies would be made available directly to the poor (perhaps through a lender); furthermore, it would permit a cen-
trally directed integration of housing units and families
in different economic brackets.

As it stands now, the costs for any number of public
improvements are being borne by particular types of devel-
opers--that is, developers of single-family subdivisions.
In a New Jersey community, for example, the local government requires such developers to install and pay for (1)
street improvements, including clearing and grading, paving,
curbs, sidewalks, storm drainage, shade trees, street-name
signs, fire hydrants, underground electric lines, and
monuments; (2) the water supply, including water mains,
service laterals, and meters; (3) sewage disposal facilities,
including sewer mains, laterals, and manholes; and (4)
land dedication for and improvements of public open space.[16]
In practice, subdivision developers may make other contributions to the community as well, as part of the process
of negotiating the best possible arrangement with local
government officials. But developers of other kinds of
land use, such as apartment houses or commercial office
buildings, are usually not required to bear heavy public
improvement costs. There is a matter of equity here (it
also may be a legal issue under the Equal Protection clause
of the Constitution) that could be overcome if local government shouldered some of the burden of the subdivision developer.

A Strategy

In this chapter we have seen how community land-use,
housing, and building policies impose a special hardship on
those of limited economic means. We have pointed out that
communities have the task of providing decent housing, where
needed, for those thousands of service workers, laboring
people, policemen and firemen, schoolteachers, clerical
personnel, and others in relatively modest-paying posts who
are presently hurt by community regulations. If existing
local policy is discriminatory and exclusionary, and if
federal money is used to support or further that policy,
then federal resources are being used for improper ends.
This is what is happening. For instance, federal water and
sewer facility assistance is advanced to localities for use
in part by residents governed by exclusionary policies and
regulations. Federal money thus is being used to underwrite

economic segregation. Other federal activities are involved as well, including the roads grant program under which federal funds are provided to states and localities for highways servicing areas protected by discriminatory zoning, federal aid to public schools that educate the children of such areas, federal urban-planning grants that are used to chart the future of these areas, federal open-space grant funds used for the acquisition of land used by residents of these areas, and federal watershed development money that is used for flood control facilities that protect such areas. Other examples could be cited.

The federal position should be that unless community policies are revamped national funds for urban development and perhaps other local activities may be withheld. Localities have a duty to provide housing for those who need it, and local controls can be shaped to encourage and perhaps assure the construction of this housing. At least the possibility of a cut-off in federal assistance in limited areas, such as grant and loan aid for key public facilities, should be openly suggested by Washington.

The present administration is apparently in no mood to move in this direction. In a statement on land use and housing opportunities in 1971, the President put the weight of the federal government on the side of nondiscriminatory housing, but this was interpreted purely in the racial sense.[17] The White House made it clear that federal resources will not be used to require economic integration or to force localities to accept low- and moderate-income housing. In fact, however, it is equally clear that economic segregation has significant racial implications. In all likelihood, racial integration cannot come without the elimination of economic segregation; and economic segregation is not apt to subside without a revision in local land-use and related policies. It might be added that economic segregation not only affects particular racial groups but religious and ethnic groups as well.

Washington should use its authority specifically to encourage communities to adopt the sort of policies discussed in this chapter--policies that encourage diversity in development, mixed land uses, and more economical construction. For too long the national government has been satisfied to use its funds to promote sprawl, straitjacket-oriented Euclidian design, and uneconomical building. In short, national programs should be directed toward breaking down old techniques and stimulating new ones, toward a policy that is founded on growth and progress and not on the status quo, toward the creation of new opportunities and living patterns and not the preservation of existing ones, and toward the building of new communities and not the conserving of old ones.

The federal government can best attain greater housing opportunities by working with local communities. But this is not the only approach, and the states can be of some help in this respect. There is already evidence that Washington has backed the efforts in some states to develop certain statewide building regulations. The need for state legislation in this area grew out of the federal government's experience in carrying out the administration's Operation Breakthrough plan, an experimental program designed to demonstrate how housing costs can be cut and economic levels mixed through factory construction techniques and more flexible layout patterns.

The case of Florida is a good illustration. Prodded to some extent by HUD, the State of Florida passed the "Florida Factory-Built Housing Act of 1971." The Florida measure was supported by the Florida Home Builders Association, the Florida Manufactured Homes Council, and the state Department of Community Affairs; significantly, it was not opposed by the group representing mobile home manufacturers. Under this legislation local codes, where in conflict with state regulations, will be preempted. The objective is, of course, to introduce factory-built (modular) housing into communities whose codes now prevent its use. This strategy has merit. An equally desirable one is for federal authorities to seek new policies at the local level; this may be a more direct and in the long run more effective route. The communities of the nation have the power to lead us in the right direction; they do not need federal dictation in the use of this power, but at the moment they could use a bit of a federal nudge.

NOTES

1. Metropolitan Social and Economic Disparities: Implications for Intergovernmental Relations in Central Cities and Suburbs, Advisory Commission on Intergovernmental Relations (Washington, D.C.: Government Printing Office, 1965), pp. 182-93.
    2. "Breakthrough," U.S. Department of Housing and Urban Development (May 1969), Appendix B, p. 24.
    3. Current state activity in housing and urban development is discussed in John N. Kolesar, "The States and Urban Planning and Development," in Alan K. Campbell, ed.,

The States and the Urban Crisis (Englewood Cliffs, N.J.:
Prentice-Hall, 1970), pp. 114-38. See also James L. Mar-
tin, "Housing and Community Development," in Robert H.
Weber, ed., The Book of the States 1970-1971 (Lexington,
Ky.: Council of State Governments, 1970), pp. 443-54.
     4. Information in this paragraph is taken from "Here
Come the Giants," Professional Builder, August 1968, pp.
87-88, 90; and Michael Sumichrast and Sara A. Frankel,
Profile of the Builder and His Industry (Washington, D.C.:
National Association of Home Builders of the United States,
1970), p. 19.
     5. Allen D. Manvel, Local Land and Building Regula-
tion (Washington, D.C.: Government Printing Office, 1968),
p. 4.
     6. Two landmark studies were conducted in the mid-
to late-1960s that have a significant bearing on the topic
under discussion. Reports were submitted by the two study
groups in 1968. One was the National Commission on Urban
Problems, called the Douglas Commission after its chairman,
former Senator Paul H. Douglas of Illinois; the other was
the President's Committee on Urban Housing, called the
Kaiser Committee after its chairman, Edgar F. Kaiser,
president of Kaiser Industries, Inc. Both panels examined
local policies that affect housing prices and land costs.
See Building the American City, National Commission on Urban
Problems (Washington, D.C.: Government Printing Office,
1968), especially Pt. 3; and A Decent Home, The President's
Committee on Urban Housing (Washington, D.C.: Government
Printing Office, 1968), especially Pt. 7.
     7. That nonpartisan elections are likely to enhance
the fortunes of the GOP is suggested in Eugene C. Lee,
Nonpartisan Politics (Berkeley: University of California
Press, 1960); and Oliver P. Williams and Charles R. Adrian,
"The Insulation of Local Politics Under the Non-Partisan
Ballot," American Political Science Review, 53 (1959), 1052-
63.
     8. For criticism of building codes designed to protect
key labor and business interests, see Bernard J. Frieden,
"Housing and National Urban Goals: Old Policies and New
Realities," in James Q. Wilson, ed., The Metropolitan Enigma
(Garden City, N.Y.: Doubleday, 1968), pp. 209-10.
     9. For a discussion of the politics of urban renewal,
see Scott Greer, Urban Renewal and American Cities (Indian-
apolis: Bobbs-Merrill, 1965), especially chap. 4; and
Harold Kaplan, Urban Renewal Politics (New York: Columbia
University Press, 1963).
     10. For an examination of this matter in the context
of Chicago politics, see Martin Meyerson and Edward C. Ban-

field, <u>Politics, Planning, and the Public Interest</u> (New
York: The Free Press, 1955).

11.   See Martin Anderson, <u>The Federal Bulldozer, A
Critical Analysis of Urban Renewal, 1949-1962</u> (Cambridge,
Mass.:   MIT Press, 1964).   Anderson's work has been strongly
criticized in some quarters; see, for example, "Federal
Bulldozer's Fallacies," <u>Journal of Housing</u>, April 1965.

12.   Daniel J. Elazar, <u>American Federalism: A View
from the States</u>, 2d ed. (New York: Thomas Y. Crowell,
1972).

13.   The Supreme Court held in 1964 that both houses
of state legislatures had to be apportioned according to
population.   <u>Reynolds v. Sims</u>, 377 U.S. 533 (1964).

14.   One community leader in New York is quoted as saying: "I'd just like to see UDC march into some suburban
area and impose their will.   It would take a year for the
political smoke to clear and UDC would lose, not the locality."   Kolesar, "The States and Urban Planning and Development," p. 125.

15.   Vincent J. Moore, "Politics, Planning, and Power
in New York State: The Path from Theory to Reality,"
<u>Journal of the American Institute of Planners</u>, XXXVII, 2
(March 1971), 66-77.

16.   Ruth L. Mace and Warren J. Wicker, <u>Do Single-Family
Homes Pay Their Way?   A Comparative Analysis of Costs and
Revenues for Public Services</u>, Research Monograph 15 (Wash-
ington, D.C.:   Urban Land Institute, 1968), p. 30.

17.   "Statement by the President on Federal Policies
Relative to Equal Housing Opportunity," June 11, 1971, 15 pp.

5

THE CITIZENS ASSOCIATION:
THE INVISIBLE POWER
IN SUBURBAN POLITICS

A LITTLE-NOTICED POWER

One of the least noticed developments in community politics over the past two decades has been the rise of neighborhood citizens associations. These groups have become influential molders of local public policy. Although their power is largely concentrated in the land-use area, citizens groups are now key participants in community decision-making processes, seeking to shape policy to their own ends, to their own conception of community development. Municipal and suburban public officials are aware of the political clout of citizens groups and are apt to tailor their own views and stands to accommodate citizens group positions. Citizens associations have been particularly active in determining the content of land-use policy and the character of the policy-making apparatus used in planning and zoning.

One of the most fascinating points about these groups is the limited extent to which they are treated in the literature on American politics. As used here, the term "citizens association" does not refer to just any group that uses the citizens title, but to the private neighborhood association that is typically found in middle- or upper-income areas of the city and suburbs, that represents its constituents before community policy-making councils, that works to protect the neighborhood from unwanted change, and that often has built its political base on opposition to rezonings. Some of these neighborhood groups are highly organized; others are loosely or informally organized, or organized on an ad hoc basis.

No book has ever been written about this type of citizens group. Few articles on the subject can be cited, and

only infrequently are citizens groups treated in lectures
and papers on community planning and land-use processes.
Citizens associations, in other words, have been almost
systematically overlooked in scholarly and academic work.
Nevertheless, citizens groups may be the single most important force in community land-use politics, and their
influence appears to be growing with the passing of each
year.

ORGANIZED CITIZEN PARTICIPATION
IN MUNICIPAL POLITICS

The idea of organized citizen involvement in the governmental processes is, of course, not new and has deep
roots in American politics. Generally, in modern times,
it grew out of the reform movement of the late 1800s and
early 1900s, although the real impact of citizens organizations was not typically felt until later. Originally, the
citizens group was a watchdog organization, one that was
to keep close tabs on city government. In the early days,
citizens organized as a means of counteracting the influence
of political machines, bosses, and parties; citizens groups
pressed municipalities to adopt reform government and reform practices such as the city manager plan and nonpartisan
elections. Citizens groups had their origins in municipal
(as distinct from suburban) government, and it was not until
the middle of this century that the idea became popular in
suburban areas.

When it did develop, the suburban citizens group seemed
to differ in important ways from its counterpart in the
cities; it had been formed on a different constituency base
and had more specialized policy concerns. For this reason,
scholars distinguish the suburban type of citizens association from that in the central city. Incidentally, either
kind of group may be found in the city or the suburb, but
in general they respectively characterize patterns of citizen organization in these two portions of the metropolitan
area. Let us compare the city civic association with the
suburban citizens association.

CIVIC ASSOCIATIONS

Basically, two sorts of citizens groups are found in
the contemporary American metropolis--the communitywide
organization and the neighborhood-based organization. The
first may be considered a "civic" association, and the

115

second, a "citizens" association. The civic association
is more directly a part of the reform tradition, and it
typically views itself as a "good government" group, striv-
ing to ensure honesty and efficiency in local government
and to promote impartial consideration and administration
of public policy.[1] Civic groups draw their membership from
the community as a whole (not from particular neighborhoods), and this may include a central city, a county, a
suburban municipality, or a metropolitan area in its en-
tirety.

In practice, although not restricted to a particular
geographical area within the city, civic groups normally
are dominated by citizens living in upper-middle-class sections of town. Civic associations often have a paid professional staff, and they may work closely with municipal
research bureaus in carrying out their various tasks. Further, these units are likely to project a liberal or progressive image in community politics, and they are commonly
pictured as representing the public interest. At present,
some civic groups have broad-based public policy interest
while others focus attention on specific matters such as
planning, housing, or elections.

Civic groups now are found in all major American cities
and in a number of suburbs. In the initial stages of the
civic reform movement, these groups were usually in the
hands of middle-class idealists and intellectuals, but with
the passing of time the control patterns seem to have
shifted somewhat, and currently the groups are frequently
under the influence of prestigious law firms and major local
business interests. In some instances, these organizations
have provided the vehicle through which reform-minded commercial and intellectual forces worked to undermine the
lower-middle-class-based political machine. Good examples
of modern civic groups are the Allegheny Conference in
Pittsburgh and Civic Progress in St. Louis. An example of
a traditionally oriented civic group would be the Municipal
League of Seattle and King County, an organization that has
wide-ranging policy interests. More specialized civic
groups would include the planning and housing councils in
some major Eastern cities and election-watchguard units
like the Citizens' League in Detroit and the Committee of
Seventy in Philadelphia.

CITIZENS ASSOCIATIONS

Citizens associations, unlike civic groups, have neighborhood constituencies and draw their membership from spe-

116

cific geographical areas within the community and not from the locality or metropolitan region as a whole. These groups are sometimes referred to as neighborhood improvement associations.[2] It is true, though, that these neighborhood associations may be joined together in federations ranging in geographical jurisdiction from a few local neighborhoods to the boundaries of the local political subdivision or beyond, but their power base and influence are largely at the neighborhood level.

Citizens associations do not have a professional staff, although they may pay consultants and attorneys to present their case to government decision-makers. These associations are found in and limited to residential areas and are most active in the more affluent of these areas; the greatest citizens association spirit is manifest in neighborhoods of upper-middle-income single-family homes. These groups generally have an economic class base, and this tends to make them suburban phenomena. In some areas, citizens groups are not permanent organizations but are mobilized only when a particular neighborhood is threatened by change.

Again unlike civic groups, citizens associations present a somewhat conservative image, and their actual policy stands represent a status quo-minded concern for particular neighborhoods. It is true, though, that citizens groups do seek to paint a progressive and "public interest" picture of themselves. Certainly, to some people, this is in fact the picture that emerges, and citizens associations can claim a rich heritage in this regard by tying themselves to the reform and good government tradition. Nevertheless, the purpose of citizens groups is the promotion of the interests, generally economic, of specific neighborhoods, and these associations commonly serve as the principal mechanism by which neighborhood leaders press local governments for policies and decisions deemed consistent with these interests, namely the maintenance of neighborhood property values. Of course, what is or is not consistent with neighborhood interests may be open to some speculation, but it is the citizens association that will make this determination.

It should be noted that these groups may be called citizens associations or civic associations, depending on the area or neighborhood involved. Within the same community, it is possible to find some of these groups calling themselves citizens associations and other civic associations. Usually, whatever term is used will be part of the title of the group, and this title also will include the name of the geographical area encompassed in the association's boundaries--thus we have the Forest Glen Citizens Association, the Walnut Hills Civic Association, and so on.

Citizens groups may cover an area that contains from 200 to 500 families, although this figure may vary widely from one part of the nation or even the metropolitan area to another. When neighborhood associations are linked through a federation, the larger unit will, of course, have a much broader membership base--up to 8,000 to 10,000 families or more. The number of families represented by citizens associations frequently has become an important political issue, for citizens groups are apt to claim wide membership in the neighborhood or area served and to speak for all members or residents; some developer groups have challenged particular associations on these points. It is difficult for an outsider to determine exact membership figures or to learn what portion of the membership participates in citizens association policy-making, a matter treated later in this chapter. In this sense, once the facts of citizens association representation are known, the theory and practice of these groups may not be one and the same.

The internal structure of formally organized citizens associations is relatively routine, at least in the technical sense. These associations will have a president, vice-president, and secretary-treasurer. Beyond this, there may be considerable variation, although the group may have at least an executive committee and committees on zoning, roads, and education. Key decisions often are made by the executive committee, which may be composed of the president, vice-president, secretary-treasurer, and the chairmen of the zoning, roads, and education committees. The tendency in recent years has been toward an expansion in the number of officers and committee chairmen, and therefore a widening of executive committee membership. Normally, the president and/or the executive committee are important forces inside citizens associations. Citizens groups may be incorporated as nonprofit organizations, and this affords them certain legal status and protection.

OTHER TYPES OF CITIZENS ORGANIZATIONS IN THE COMMUNITY

Citizens associations should not be confused with other types of community organizations that may resemble them in certain respects. In addition to the citizens and civic associations, a number of suburban areas contain homeowners associations, and, although these groups may cover a

portion of an area served by a citizens association, the
two are not the same. Homeowners have been organized into
such groups at least as far back as 1891, and these groups
have been termed "homes associations" by some.[3]

Homeowners associations may be found in new subdivisions that contain open-space, recreational, or other public
improvements and facilities that have been deeded by the
developer to the residents. Membership in such associations
usually is not voluntary as it is with citizens associations,
and homeowners groups assess their members and administer
and maintain land, improvements, and facilities held in
common. Homeowners associations may have architectural
powers over new construction in the subdivision, enforce
private covenants, and perform other duties. According to
William H. Whyte, there are some 350 homeowners associations throughout the United States.[4]

Communities may have other citizens-type groups that
differ from the citizens association being discussed here.
Nearly all areas have government-established citizens committees. These committees normally are attached to particular local government offices (mayor, city council), agencies, or departments, and their members are often appointed
by the mayor, city or county manager or executive, or the
local governing body. Appointees to citizens committees
usually serve for specified terms; such committees may be
permanent or ad hoc. The powers of government-created
citizens committees vary widely, although it is likely that
most are advisory. The scope of the formal interests of
citizens committees also varies.

Citizens committees differ from citizens associations
in three important ways: (1) citizens committees do not
usually have a neighborhood base, being drawn from the community at large; (2) citizens committees have a governmental
character; and (3) citizens committee members serve by appointment. Citizens associations serve only neighborhoods,
are not governmental in character, and are not appointive
organizations. At the same time, both citizens committees
and citizens associations may serve as vehicles by which
particular interests influence public policy.

One of the most marked tendencies in recent years has
been the development of lower-socioeconomic area neighborhood citizens organizations. These organizations normally
are found in central cities, but they exist in some suburbs
as well. Some of these groups have arisen out of the yeoman
work of the late Saul Alinsky, well-known community orga-
nizer; Alinsky was responsible for The Woodlawn Organization,
which operates in a Chicago slum, and he organized other

such groups in other areas.[5]   But, more often, citizens organizations in low-income neighborhoods have been stimu-
lated by federally backed activities like the community action and model cities programs.

Low-income neighborhood citizens organizations differ
in key ways from the suburban neighborhood citizens association. First, the former normally have been created
largely, perhaps exclusively, because of outside pressure
or leadership; they have not developed in the more natural
fashion characteristic of the suburban citizens association. Second, they serve lower-income neighborhoods and
not the middle-income or wealthier areas containing the
citizens associations. Third, there is every indication
that poverty neighborhood organizations are controlled
from outside the neighborhood by middle-class interests in
such diverse organizations as a community action agency,
chamber of commerce, city planning department, civil rights
group, city council, model cities agency, or a local university. Although decisions in suburban citizens associations are commonly made by a small elite, it is a home-
grown elite and not imported from outside the area.

Significantly, there is far more information in the
literature of political science on organizations of citizens
in the slums than there is on suburban citizens associations.[6]
Yet it seems safe to say that the influence, particularly
the independent influence, of the latter goes well beyond
that of the former.

CITIZENS ASSOCIATIONS AS
INTEREST GROUPS

There has been much discussion in academic and planning
circles throughout the country about whether community-
level citizens organizations should have a private interest
or public interest base.[7] (In fact, this is largely an
academic matter, for whether a citizens group does or does
not have a private interest base essentially is determined
empirically and not by philosophical discussions.) Typically, planners and academic spokesmen argue that the only
legitimate way to form such an organization is on public
interest grounds. This conception is certainly consistent
with the reform and good-government view that provided the
philosophical base of the earlier municipal civic groups.
This view pictures citizens groups as a positive force, promoting the collective interests of the community as a
whole, not as a negative instrument, protecting the special
interests--especially the economic interests--of a few.

At the same time, others such as Alinsky hold that the only effective foundation of neighborhood groups is self-interest. This would include the interest that the neighborhood has in protecting itself from outside forces and influences that work against it. To Alinsky, the neighborhood organization must be founded and operate on a base of power, power that is respected outside the neighborhood. Alinsky contended that it is power, interest, and money that make community politics tick. According to this analysis, it is only reasonable and natural that neighborhood interests seek to play the political game the only way that it can be played successfully—by mobilizing these resources themselves. Alinsky, it should be pointed out parenthetically, was wary of government-spawned organizations, and considered them a contradiction in terms in low-income neighborhoods that are not represented in the government in the first place (suggesting manipulation by outside interests, to the advantage of others, not the poor). Alinsky was generally distrustful of traditional power structures under any circumstances, whether in government or business.[8]

Whether one accepts Alinsky's or the more commonly heard "public interest" arguments, it would seem that the suburban type of citizens association is closer to the Alinsky self-interest than the public interest model. Suburban citizens associations are generally self-interest organizations and operate on the premise that power, especially in numbers, can and should dictate public policy. Moreover, this self-interest and power have a special neighborhood and economic focus and are not drawn from the broader communitywide scheme of things. To the citizens association, neighborhood interests must be protected; the association is the vehicle through which this viewpoint is transmitted to community decision-makers.

Although one normally thinks of Washington, or perhaps of the state capital, when discussing interest groups, such organizations are also active at the community level. Citizens associations have not always been seen as interest groups. This is beginning to change, and it now is not unheard of for texts in state and local government to consider neighborhood citizens associations to be interest groups. One leading scholar defines an interest group (which he calls a pressure group) as "an organized aggregate which seeks to influence the content of governmental decisions without attempting to place its members in formal governmental capacities."[9] The latter part of this definition is designed to exclude political parties. An introductory political science text views interest groups as "any private, nonpartisan group of people who seek to influence some phase of public policy."[10] By either definition, the suburban citizens association qualifies as an interest group: it is a private organization, nonpartisan in nature, that has as a goal the desire to shape public policy, mostly community land-use policy; and, unlike parties, it does not exist to secure government posts for its members.

In some parts of the country, neighborhoods are not formally organized into citizens associations but are still active in protecting neighborhood interests. Formally organized or not, neighborhoods constitute an interest group if they act politically as neighborhoods, seeking to protect neighborhood interests in political and governmental councils. To qualify as an interest group, it is not necessary to be formally, permanently, or even openly organized --only to act collectively, on a matter that concerns all so acting, within a political or governmental framework.[11]

Interest groups can be divided further into public interest groups and private interest groups. Public interest groups additionally can be subdivided into organizations that represent governments or public officials, such as the U.S. Conference of Mayors (represents big-city mayors) or the National Governors' Conference, and groups that represent broadly based interests, such as the Urban Coalition and Common Cause. Public interest groups represent government or broadly based interests. Private interest groups, on the other hand, represent particular forces in the private sector; examples are labor unions and business trade groups (chambers of commerce, manufacturers association builders groups).

It is reasonable to argue that citizens associations fall in the private interest group category. Citizens associations are moved by the special interests of residents of particular neighborhoods, are founded on an economic base, and operate in a manner virtually identical with the more generally recognized specialized interest groups found at all levels of the political system. To be considered public interest groups, citizens associations would either have to be governments (which, of course, they are not) or represent the interests of the people generally (which they do not). Thus they do not differ from their chief rivals, builder-developer organizations, long recognized as private interest groups with important economic stakes in politics.

THE HISTORY OF SUBURBAN CITIZENS ASSOCIATIONS

The sort of citizens group that is treated in this chapter traces its roots to the mid- and late-1940s. It was at the end of World War II that the out-migration from cities became noticeable and that the political effects of the movement to the suburbs became marked, although the suburban exodus was well under way by this time (suburban areas had been growing faster than cities since the decade 1920-30).[12] In the postwar period, suburban government incorporations surged, special districts to handle new functions in the suburbs were created, preexisting suburban municipalities, counties, townships, and towns were politically strengthened, reformers began making suburban inroads, suburban bosses were toppled, suburbs switched to council-manager governments, and suburban citizens associations were formed.

However, unlike the civic association in the cities, the suburban citizens association was not so concerned about "good government" or "honest elections" as abstract matters. These groups were created mainly for defensive purposes; they were started as protective associations. Their ends from the very beginning were more negative than positive, and they were formed not so much to promote progress as to stop it. Their political posture was and remains one of opposition to change, opposition to new land uses, opposition to variety and diversity. The citizens associations represented a new mood in American politics, one based on the preservation of home investments in the neighborhood. Citizens groups picture themselves in a more favorable light, as protectors of the environment and preservers of neighborhood character.

In implementing their political and economic philosophy, citizens associations from the early days have concentrated on defeating rezoning efforts. In addition to working against particular rezoning requests, their initial strategy was to back like-minded candidates for public office. This meant that their attention was directed at the community governing body, a popularly elected group that had the final authority on zoning matters. This strategy apparently proved effective, and, by the late 1950s and early 1960s, community after community had fallen into the hands of citizens association forces and their sympathizers. In the 1940s, most of the 1950s, and later in some places, the local elected leadership seemed more inclined to favor the business and real estate point of view, more willing to grant rezonings, more concerned about strengthening the tax base with economically productive uses, and more sensitive to market demands for physical, social, and economic change. This reflected the power of real estate groups at the time.

In the early years, citizens groups appeared to concern themselves less with the planning commission than with the

governing board. In any event, they were less successful
in gaining a political foothold on planning boards than they
were in influencing elected bodies. Of course, planning
boards are appointed for specified terms, not elected, and
therefore presumably not as subject to citizens group pressure. Planning commissions thus have been among the last
of the major land-use control agencies in local government
to succumb to citizens association domination or influence.

THE CONTEMPORARY SUBURBAN
CITIZENS ASSOCIATION

Today, in any number of suburban municipalities and
counties, neighborhood-based citizens associations reign
unchallenged in their area of interest. Their influence
has widened considerably over the years, and they now typically focus much attention on the general planning process
in addition to rezonings. The idea is that if citizen
groups can build their principles into the plan in the
first place it will not be necessary for them to wage such
continuing battles on particular zoning matters. If the
plan can be shaped according to the doctrines of preserving
the interests of existing neighborhoods and the widespread
extension of a single-family residential uses into new and
undeveloped areas, those wanting to introduce variety in
land uses will have to overcome an important additional ob-
stacle--the plan.
A typical citizens group approach has been to support
plans that call for the preservation of large areas of open-
space wedges in the rural or essentially rural portions of
the suburbs. This appears to be lofty objective, but the
evidence suggests that citizens groups may favor this sort
of plan not because they want open space for any particular
environmental reason and not because they anticipate estate
or large-lot development (which will likely occur), but because they are convinced that it will bring a halt to development altogether; this they favor because they believe
that it keeps taxes lower; because it keeps others, especially low-income and minority ethnic groups, out of the
community; and because it protects existing property values.
Whether citizens association reasoning on this matter is
correct or not is unimportant, it is only important that the
reasoning is believed. It does not seem that citizens associations want new residents who are much (if at all)
wealthier than current residents, and they certainly oppose
new residents who are poorer than the present ones. To the

citizens group, the designation of open wedges on the plan
assures the exclusion of all new people and all new development. This is often the citizens association conception
of a well-planned community. Such groups may end up supporting a plan that brings in only affluent neighbors, as
a sort of reluctant concession to reality.

Citizens association positions on public policy seldom
change from the time the group originally is formed. Citizens groups, in fact, often have come into being as a result of a specific threat to the neighborhood--usually a
proposed change in land use in the area or the proposed
location of a highway through the neighborhood. The introduction of a new force--new residents, new business, new
land uses, new transportation--into the neighborhood constitutes a threat, and the force is to be repelled. The
citizens association sits as a kind of armed guard, protecting the neighborhood from new influences and serving as a
screening mechanism determining who may enter the neighborhood and on what terms. Its posture remains constant and
unchanged as the years pass.

That the citizens association does not have the power
of government causes it to seek the next best thing--control
over the public powers in the community that affect the
neighborhood. This, of course, puts citizens groups in the
midst of politics. But it is likely to be private politics,
for the decision-makers who act formally in the name of
the public, formally to advance the public interest, formally to protect the general welfare, are often in reality
simply ratifying decisions made previously by neighborhood
citizens groups. That citizens associations put pressure
on local government to make land-use and other decisions
consistent with the stands of the associations is hardly
disputable; neither is the fact that the citizens association position frequently prevails in government councils.
In a sense, this is the best of all possible worlds for
citizens groups since they can wield power over the content
and timing of government decisions but do not have to take
the public responsibility for making them.

Citizens associations often oppose neighborhood master
plans that provide for high-density housing or for the possibility of low-income housing and commercial uses. When
the community adopts a neighborhood master plan that is exclusionary in its economic, racial, and business effects,
when the community votes down a rezoning that would provide
for any of these uses, it is the governing body and the
planning commission that take the action in the formal
sense, not the citizens association. Thus, if the community

is criticized from the outside, the finger is pointed at the elected and appointed officials of government, not at the citizens association. All may end up pointing the finger at developers for not providing the needed uses (low-income housing is a good example), when in reality the citizens association has been preventing such development all along. Public officials rarely are willing to admit that they are influenced by citizens associations, for this suggests they are subject to pressures.

This discussion is not intended to suggest that citizens associations are the only "interest groups" seeking to shape government actions, for, as noted earlier, developers and other real estate interests are organized for the same purpose. However, the citizens group pressure and developer influence differ markedly in their consequences for land-use policy.

Public Policy Interests

Citizens associations have an interest in land use, highways, and education. These three issues can be expected to take up to 80 percent or more of the time citizens groups spend on public policy. These interests go somewhat beyond the typical listing of specific substantive issues of concern to the suburbs: schools and land use.[13] Highways are of greater interest to citizens associations than to suburbs generally because of the critical matter of road location. The suburbs of the nation seem to be generally convinced that highways are needed, particularly the arterial type that lead into the central city. Highways as such have not been a matter of suburban controversy (at least until the last couple of years). But the particular location of roads in the suburbs, especially major highways, is a matter of great moment to some citizens associations. We shall discuss citizens association interests in highways first, then turn to schools, and finally to land use, the chief concern. The position that citizens associations take on highways is something akin to their position on housing the poor; they favor it in principle, but not in their neighborhoods. Yet there is an important difference here as well, for citizens associations usually do in fact favor highways; their dedication to housing the poor is less clear. That is, although citizens associations work against major highways running through their neighborhoods, they do in reality want these highways built—built elsewhere, but built. Suburban residents in single-family subdivisions need major

highways to get to their places of business and to travel
to shopping, entertainment, and cultural centers. Citizen
assocation members use highways, but they do not use low-
income housing. In one case, a citizens association was
not satisfied to go on record as opposing an arterial highway planned for its neighborhood; it also passed a resolution supporting the same highway in another (lower-income)
neighborhood some miles away. In addition to opposing new
highways, citizens groups often lobby against changes in
existing ones, especially road widenings.

As the environmental issue becomes more prominent, it
is likely that suburban citizens associations will work it
into their roads policy and highway location stands. Some
already have. Evidence suggests that citizens associations
may become allies of the more broadly based antifreeway
forces in some areas, drawing on the environmental tag used
by these forces, but using it as an instrument to strike
at specific unwanted roads. If this takes place, freeway
opponents probably will not be able to count on the support
of citizens associations except when highways threaten particular neighborhoods. Highways are not an ideological
issue to most citizens associations (although highways may
be supported "ideologically" by some association members),
and neither is any other issue. Particular highways are
opposed because they threaten a neighborhood, assocation
members' economic interests, and property values. The opposition is based on quite practical considerations.

But fighting roads does not take that much time on the
agenda of the typical citizens association, and such a
threat may occur only infrequently if at all. Even less
time is devoted to schools, not because education is an
unimportant matter but because middle- and upper-income
neighborhoods delegate this task to the PTA and perhaps
other groups. Unlike the citizens association, the PTA represents part of the local government bureaucracy (teachers)
as well as neighborhood citizens (parents). The nature of
representation in the PTA may subject this organization to
greater bureaucratic influence than is the case with the
purely and simply citizen-controlled citizens association.[14]

Citizens associations may be concerned about the location of new public schools and the expansion or modification
of the physical plant of existing schools. Citizens groups
also may be drawn into the politics of the suburban school
system on other matters, particularly when one of the more
permanent participants in school government processes needs
outside political support. The permanent participants in
suburban educational politics may include the school system

hierarchy (school board, school system administrators), schoolteachers, the PTA, nonpartisan organizations concerned with public education, and public officials outside of the school bureaucracy. The PTA would be the most likely to seek citizens group assistance, as there may be overlap in the leadership of the neighborhood citizens association and that of the PTA.

Yet roads and schools together do not constitute the major focal points of citizens associations. The most time and the greatest attention is reserved for land use--and this essentially means zoning, the number one concern. Citizens associations concentrate their attention on zoning for the same reason that developers and most other participants in suburban land-use politics do--zoning policy determines the basic patterns of land development. Planning, of course, is not irrelevant to these patterns, but it is more likely to come after the fact if indeed at all. This is not to suggest that suburban citizens associations have no interest in planning, for it already has been suggested how planning is used by these groups to foster their own conception of proper community development. But citizens associations know that the real battles in suburban land-use politics are over zoning, and that those interests prevailing in the zoning arena will set the pace and dictate the future of community development.

It is not an overstatement to say that most citizens associations exist primarily for the purpose of defeating rezonings.* The politics of zoning basically pits the developer against the citizens association interests. Mainly to strengthen their hand in this conflict, citizens associations have formed subfederations and federations. This is not a departure from the neighborhood orientation of citizens associations, for the purpose of this sort of alliance is to bolster the political position of the neighborhood group. The most important political resource that citizens associations have is numbers (membership or support), and the greater the number of families that can be cited in opposition to particular rezonings the more impressed public officials are apt to be. Through a federation, the resources of all member associations can be used in any particular rezoning issue.

---

*This applies to "special exceptions" to zoning regulations as well, particularly those that have effects similar to rezonings.

Thus with a federation, a member association can claim that 10,000 instead of 200 to 500 families are opposed to a particular measure. Federation and subfederation resources often are used to back assertions and positions of neighborhood affiliates; the neighborhood focus is therefore not lost.

In general, citizens associations can be expected to work against any significant change in land use in their neighborhoods. They will oppose changes in zoning from residential to commercial, from residential to industrial, from low-density residential to high-density residential, and from large-lot residential to small-lot residential. Not that this covers all zonings opposed by citizens groups, but these represent the most common ones. Until recently, rezoning requests were virtually exclusively of the variety presented here, although lately a number of communities have been rezoning in the other direction—that is, to low-density residential uses, a process commonly referred to as "up-zoning" (see Chapter 3). "Up-zoning" is not initiated by landowners, as is the more traditional form of rezoning. Up-zoning stacks the cards against landowners and developers and creates barriers to development; citizens associations commonly back up-zoning, and once land is so zoned, they return to their typical position in opposition to zoning changes.

Other than up-zoning, what does the citizens association support? Is there anything the citizens association is _for_? Yes. Citizens groups may lend their support to master plans, even the kind that call for needed public and commercial facilities, needed high-density residential uses, and varied land uses. But this support is often short-lived, and it may not be all that meaningful in the final analysis because plans do not control development. What happens in practice? Plans are drawn up on the basis of the broader interests of the community. These plans are discussed with the residents and may be adopted by the planning commission and perhaps the governing body, with the general backing of the citizens groups. But at the point of implementation, particularly when a rezoning is requested to carry out the plan, the citizens association frequently reneges. It is at this point that the citizens association so commonly reverts to its typical operational style and becomes the opposition force.

The reasons for this apparent inconsistency are not entirely clear, but it would seem that citizens groups are guilty of not practicing what they preach, of not following in fact when they say they approve of in theory. In theory, variety and diversity sound fine, but apparently they have less appeal in reality. In theory, meeting the needs of the broader community for public and commercial facilities is a worthy end, but in practice it cannot be permitted. At least this is the impression one gets.

There is certainly not a citizens association that does not recognize the need for commercial facilities near residential neighborhoods. There is not a citizens group anywhere that does not agree that public services and facilities should be located where they can be used by community residents. And no citizens association disagrees with the proposition that housing should be provided for all people who need it. That is, they do not disagree in the abstract, and plans may be abstract. The problem arises when someone attempts to make the abstraction a reality.

Another factor is important in this regard. A zoning change that is required to effect a plan has immediate and direct implications for particular pieces of property and for particular existing residents. A plan has no such implications and therefore may not pose any meaningful challenge to present development patterns. In practical terms, a specific proposal to build a particular commercial facility on a particular lot (zoning) is quite a different matter from proposing future commercial uses in several areas within the community (plan). The first is taken seriously and opposed; the second is not taken seriously and is supported.

One of the most fascinating aspects of the whole attitude of the suburban citizens association toward zoning and planning is the inequity of it all. It was frequently a change in zoning that permitted the citizens association members to get into the suburbs in the first place. Yet, when it comes time to open up new areas for development, when it comes time for the suburbs to take their share of new commercial and higher-density housing uses, the citizens association says no. Citizens groups seem to be suggesting: we made it, and we want to make darned sure that others do not. And there is little doubt that the ultimate goal is no new development. Development is opposed per se, and any means that attain this goal are considered acceptable. Nothing is overlooked in the search for exclusionary devices; no possibility is left untried. The search for tools to restrict development is a continual one.

The most common antidevelopment tools are zoning and planning. There is another vehicle though--and that is sewers. Not satisfied with open-wedge planning and low-density zoning as devices to stop development, citizens

groups have turned their attention to sewer extensions.
Citizens associations have sought to pressure government
officials into refusing to extend sewers into undeveloped
and rural areas of the suburbs. Where no legitimate way can
be found to stop sewer extensions altogether, citizens
groups may propose limited-access sewers. The operation of
the sewer system is normally a local government function
(often under special districts, a form of local government),
and it is well known that developers depend on sewers to
service new subdivisions. Without public sewers nearby,
development is apt to be uneconomical (private sewerage
systems are costly to the developer), lot sizes must typically be larger (for health and zoning reasons), and thus
land is more likely to remain in an undeveloped state.

In some communities, basic decisions on sewer extensions are considered to be part of land-use policy. These
decisions would have to do with interceptor and trunk sewers, or whatever the community considers to be its major
sanitary sewers. Without public sewers, private sewerage
systems must be installed to service particular developments or septic tanks must be used. The concern here is
not so much with sewage disposal facilities (physical plant)
as with sewer lines that ultimately connect homes and businesses with these facilities. Limited-access sewers can be
used only for highly specialized purposes (perhaps for a
particular government installation) and citizens and developers along the way may be denied use of such sewers, regardless of proximity or need. A "no-sewer" or "limited-
access-sewer" policy casts sewers into an openly political
role.

Sewers would seem to be the last matter to be made an
overt political issue, but they have been made one and
promise to remain one in the future. In the past, sewers
were viewed in a purely technical light, serving as a means
of disposing liquid waste and promoting sanitary living
conditions. In sewer extension decision-making, the only
consideration besides cost was need, not effect on development. If politics was involved, it was involved only in
the administration of the sewer department or district,
and then confined to personnel, patronage, or contract matters. Now sewers are seen differently--at least by citizens
groups. Sewers are seen as a land-use control, a tool for
shaping development in desired patterns. Of course, there
is little question that sewer policy significantly affects
the character of future development,[15] or that developers
knew this long before citizens groups did (and acted accord-
ingly, politically).

There is another important land-use control tool: subdivision regulation. Subdivision control is listed last because citizens associations are not particularly interested in it. Subdivision control policy is primarily a matter between the developer and the local government, especially the agency principally responsible for administering subdivision regulations (often the planning commission). Zoning sets the basic tone of development, and the subdivision power is not likely to alter this to any extent. If, however, the subdivision ordinance permits any important deviation from zoning, the citizens association is apt to get involved in subdivision regulation administration. This is particularly true if any clustering is proposed, or if any changes in the front-, side-, and back-yard setbacks are planned. In other words, any departure from the conventional suburban residential zoning practice of one house per lot with wide setback requirements is apt to draw citizens association interest. Citizens association concern usually is directed toward particular subdivision plans (for specific tracts of land), not the subdivision ordinance itself.

LEGITIMATE INTERESTS OF CITIZENS ASSOCIATIONS

Do citizens associations have legitimate interests to protect? The answer has to be that they do. Citizens groups represent important neighborhood interests, largely economic in character. That citizens groups would form around these interests is natural, and this pattern conforms to the nature of the American political system. This is not a new phenomenon.

The interests that citizens associations represent are private. Private interests can be protected under our system of politics, and interest groups are commonly formed to protect such interests. The residents of neighborhoods have a perfect right to band together to protect their investments. For homeowners, the investment that is made in the home is frequently a substantial one. In any event, owners have an important stake in their homes, an economic one. Public policy clearly affects home values and therefore the investments people have in homes. Land-use and highway policies are particularly relevant in this regard, and homeowners have every reason to seek to influence such policies so that the desired economic effect is achieved. The desired economic effect is the maintenance and perhaps the appreciation of home values. Public policy, especially

zoning, can cause property values in the neighborhood to
rise, drop, or remain steady.

However, it is the rare citizens association that stops
at this point, or even concedes that it exists primarily or
entirely to protect the economic interests of its members.
Citizens groups typically wrap themselves in public interest garb and seek to dress up their legitimate interests
as something more than they are. This, it can be argued,
is objectionable and somewhat deceptive, although not unusual.

One also may question just how far the protection of
neighborhood economic interests can go. Does the need to
protect these interests give citizens groups the right to
dictate what homes, if any, others will have? Is this necessary to protect these interests? Does the need to protect
these interests give citizens groups the right to stipulate
the zoning of land throughout the community, to impose
their values on others who are more directly affected? Is
this strategically necessary, given the legitimate interests
of citizens associations? Is it necessary to the protection
of neighborhood interests for citizens groups to determine
who will and will not be allowed access to public sewers,
regardless of need or health and pollution considerations?

Citizens associations, like other groups, certainly
are entitled to their views, however offensive they may be
to others. But it is questionable whether they have to or
should be encouraged to shape public policy in the community
to accord with these views--shape it, that is, beyond the
degree needed to protect the economic interests of their
members. One can hardly underestimate the ultimate effects
of citizens association rule on the entire metropolitan
area and the nation as a whole. Although these groups indi-
vidually may represent only a few hundred families, when
one considers the total number of such groups and that they
form an impenetrable circle around many central cities, the
implications of their political power and its exercise are
enormous. These implications are not limited to the suburbs.

CITIZENS ASSOCIATION REPRESENTATIVENESS

Students of local politics have long studied community
influence and decision-making patterns. Two broad sets of
conclusions have emerged. Sociologists, in the main, have
concluded that American communities are ruled by a social
and economic elite, that the influence of this elite extends
to all major issues in the community, and that political

and governmental leaders are subordinate to this elite.[16]
Political scientists, on the other hand, generally have
concluded that communities contain different power centers,
that no single elite dominates all issue areas (even the
major ones), that political and governmental leaders are
key participants in the decision-making process, and that
power is distributed among several groups, not concentrated
in one.[17] Yet little attention has been given to the patterns of influence and the decision-making processes inside
private groups that are only part of the community power
structure.

In general, what information there is on internal decision-making in interest groups points in the direction of
elite control. Seymour Martin Lipset notes the existence
of oligarchic rule in interest groups and indicates that
the principal justifications for this are that it better
allows interest groups to compete in the political struggle
and bargain with others, and that internal democracy and
conflict are not necessary since only a single interest is
represented.[18] However, one marked disadvantage of elitist
rule within interest groups is that the group will not represent the true interests of its members.

At the community level, Wallace S. Sayre and Herbert
Kaufman discovered that civic groups in New York City were
run by a small group of activists whose tenure spanned
long periods of time.[19] Every indication is that Sayre's
and Kaufman's findings are not peculiar to New York.

Suburban neighborhood citizens associations typically
are controlled by a small elite who make all key decisions
and who act in the name of the general membership. This
small group commonly will include five to ten persons, who
may comprise the executive committee of the association.
Decisions often are reached informally and then announced
through the appropriate formal channels. There is little
evidence to suggest that the decisions of the controlling
elite are ratified by the general membership, except perhaps in the loosest of fashions.

One way of going about gathering data about the degree
of representativeness found in suburban citizens associations is to ask public officials who deal with these associations on a continuing basis. One study did this.[20] It
examined the attitudes of planning commission and governing
body members in two major suburban jurisdictions on the
East Coast. Officials were interviewed and asked to indicate the extent to which they agreed or disagreed with certain propositions on land-use, planning, and zoning matters.
(Not of concern here, these attitudes then were compared

to the officials' voting record to determine the degree of consistency.) The responses to statements on citizens associations were as follows:

"The public would be better served if the planning commission almost consistently followed the advice of local citizens associations."

	Number of Officials
Strongly agree	0
Agree	2
Disagree	14
Strongly disagree	14

"Citizens associations generally represent the public on planning questions."

	Number of Officials
Strongly agree	0
Agree	18
Disagree	7
Strongly disagree	5

It is instructive to note that not one official "strongly agreed" and that only two officials "agreed" with the proposition that the public would be better served if planners heeded the advice of citizens associations. In all, 28 of the 30 officials interviewed could not accept this point of view and were split evenly between those who "disagreed" and those who "strongly disagreed." On the second matter, no official "strongly agreed" that citizens groups generally represent the public in planning, but 18 "agreed"; a substantial minority, 12, either "disagreed" or "strongly disagreed." In comparing the responses to the two statements, one might speculate that suburban officials feel that citizens associations should not be permitted to control land-use policy even if they are representative of the public. Yet the fact remains that 40 percent of the officials interviewed did not believe that citizens associations represent the public.

Another study conducted by a recognized polling organization addressed the question of citizens association representativeness. By way of background, a federation of neighborhood citizens associations in a major suburban jurisdiction took a stand on an important land-use matter. The federation claimed to represent 8,000 families--the sum total of the membership of 12 constituent citizens groups. The polling organization then talked to a representative sample of residents in the areas served by the neighborhood associations who belonged to the federation. The results showed that less than 3 percent of the residents knew that the federation existed, and only about 1 percent had any knowledge of the position the federation had taken on the issue being considered.

Of course the number of residents in an area served by a citizens association and the number of members of that citizens association are not one and the same; it appears, however, that citizens groups do not always make this distinction. Also, there is considerable debate over citizens association membership figures. In the first place, it is not clear how many "members" can legitimately be considered such. For example, how many "members" currently are paying dues, certainly one important criterion of membership? Further, how many "members" actually attend meetings, certainly an indication of active involvement? Second, regardless of claims to the contrary, it is likely that membership figures are not static, that they rise and fall, and rather dramatically, according to the presence of a threat to the neighborhood. While membership figures undoubtedly swell during periods of crisis (a proposed rezoning or road in the neighborhood), these figures are likely to be much lower under normal circumstances. It is not clear that the lower (and probably typical) membership figures are considered by association leadership. Third, when citizens associations form federations, they usually feel that it is not necessary for the federation to back up membership claims since federations are not direct-membership organizations (as neighborhood groups are). Thus federations are in the convenient position of using the larger (collective) membership figures, adding the power of numbers to the stands they take but not having to produce evidence of this membership (only neighborhood associations have this information, and they are not directly involved here).

One indication of the degree of community support for an organization is the willingness of its members to contribute financially to it. In the case of citizens associations, this would be reflected in the extent to which community residents are willing to back these groups with financial resources. While there are exceptions to this, citizens associations generally are not well funded; and although

they may hire experts, consultants, and attorneys to represent them, their record of meeting the financial obligations
they incur does not appear to be especially good. The reason for this, if true, is their inability to raise the money
in the community; this suggests somewhat passive support at
best among neighborhood residents.

In sum, it seems that most sympathizers as well as
opponents of neighborhood citizens associations accept un-
critically the assumption that citizens groups represent
the citizens and the public in particular areas if not in
general. The facts point to the conclusion that this assumption may be unwarranted, at least without significant
qualifications and reservations. Citizens groups represent
themselves as much as they represent the citizens; they
represent the leadership as much as the membership.

CITIZENS ASSOCIATION RELATIONS WITH
OTHER COMMUNITY GROUPS

Citizens Associations and Parties

Citizens associations are nonpartisan organizations.
They are not political parties but interest groups. In
searching out partners in politics, they are not choosy
about party labels. They will work with any party that
helps advance their ends, they will work with whatever party
is in power, they will switch from one party to another if
this serves their interests, and they will seek to exert
influence on any party that is found in the community.
Citizens associations primarily are concerned with preserving the self-interests of the neighborhoods they represent;
all other matters are subordinate and must fit into this
general scheme. They resemble other interest groups, including developers, in this respect.

In partisan communities in the North, citizens groups
generally work most closely with the Republican party, although those in cities or those located in industrial suburbs may cooperate with the local Democratic organization.
In the border states and the South, citizens groups are apt
to work through the Democratic party, which is frequently
in control in both the cities and the suburbs.

In all parts of the country, citizens groups are more
likely to work with liberals than conservatives in both
parties. This is particularly so where Republican and
Democratic conservatives have been associated with landown-

137

ing interests. If a community has two parties (Republican and Democrat) and if one or both parties have two wings split along conservative-liberal lines, citizens associations may attempt to strengthen their political hand by gaining control of the liberal faction of each party. In a number of cases though, there is for all intents and purposes only one party (Republican in the North, Democratic in the South), and often there is a dominant faction or controlling interest in that party. In such instances, citizens groups will deal with this controlling faction, if this is possible, and may in fact provide much of the political base for the ruling party interest; if this is not possible, citizens groups may support a dissident faction and seek to oust the controlling interests.

In one sense political parties obviously are "used" by citizens groups, but parties may have something to gain as well. Parties like to rule, at least formally, and this causes them to seek out important support and to line up with key community interests. In localities, citizens groups may be the most powerful interest around, and parties may want to forge alliances with these groups in this light. In dealing with citizens associations, the party and particular party officeholders or officeseekers have much to gain because of the visibility and credit they get for making (in the formal sense) public decisions. The party and party leaders may in other words ride to power on the backs of citizens associations. The citizens associations may get the benefits of the decisions made by government and the party, but the party has the legal control of the organs of government. Both may "win" in the bargain, and this sort of trade-off is the essence of suburban politics in many areas. This kind of suburban politics is no different in principle from the big-city politics of the past, although the former is less open. In both instances, the parties are expected to "pay off" in return for the right to rule; in cities this meant municipal jobs for the party faithful and contracts and licenses for business, while in the suburbs it means favorable land-use and zoning decisions (from the citizens association point of view).

Many suburban communities have nonpartisan elections, and the local government is not run by one of the two major parties. In these areas, there may be local parties or groups (not Republican or Democratic) that serve to mobilize the electorate and operate the government. Citizens groups appear to be more successful in controlling land-use policy in nonpartisan communities than partisan ones. In some situations the local party is little more than a confederation of neighborhood citizens groups, and neighborhood citizens group interests may form the political backbone for this party, provide manpower for the party at election time, and guide the party's land-use policy stances between elections. In return, the local party enacts residential zoning on a widespread basis, turns down requests for rezoning, opposes business and commercial zoning, and in general works for low-density residential development. There may be considerable overlap in leadership in citizens groups and local parties, serving to blend the two forces into one.

Citizens Associations and Developers

In their quest for political partners, citizens groups have not courted developers. The mere thought sends most citizens association leaders into a tizzy. Citizens groups often picture developers as evil and view them as profit-seekers who disregard community interests, ruin the environment, and disrupt neighborhoods with their schemes. They are the enemy, and one does not deal with them. And citizens associations, it seems, cooperate only with officials who have a known antideveloper record.

Citizens Associations and
Chambers of Commerce

It should be noted, however, that citizens associations are not entirely without allies in the business community, at least on particular land-use matters. Citizens associations and local chambers of commerce (or boards of trade) may find themselves on the same side of some land-use questions. Both, for example, may oppose specific rezonings for commercial purposes. They may be opposed for different reasons, but they may nevertheless be united in their opposition. The chamber of commerce is apt to be opposed to new commercial zoning for competitive reasons. Zoning that may create competition for present businesses, especially rezonings for major new shopping and commercial concentrations, may draw the fire of local organized business. This is not to suggest that all new business zoning is opposed by organized business--only that it may be.

The chamber of commerce in the community represents existing businesses, those that already have a stake in the community, those with more or less stable clientele. And existing businesses sometimes feel that they have much to lose if zoning permitting new business is approved. The chamber of commerce typically will back zoning that produces more customers (most residential zoning) but is not of one mind on commercial zoning. In practice, the chamber of commerce may be as protective and defensive in political posture as citizens associations. The link between the chamber and citizens associations may not be a direct or permanent one, and may be more a matter of mutual interests surrounding particular zoning decisions than anything else.

CONSEQUENCES OF CITIZENS ASSOCIATION RULE

Citizens associations have sought to turn the land-use policy processes into decision-making by plebiscite. No matter what public arguments they use in backing their political stands, citizens groups attempt to make it abundantly clear that public officials who fail to respond favorably to association demands will be defeated at the polls. They also make it clear that appointed officials who want new appointments or higher positions had better toe the citizens association line. In effect, citizens groups are saying that public decision-makers should take action based on what the groups feel the largest number of people want at the moment or suffer the consequences. This is not an idle threat, for citizens groups can and do mobilize the public for these disciplinary purposes. This they see as the democratic answer to the developers' money, which is used to influence political decisions on land use.

But are citizens groups the only interests that should be represented in community land-use decision-making? Even if citizens groups are telling us the truth when they claim that they represent the people, should we have zoning and land-use control purely by plebiscite--by vote representative only of existing residents of small geographical areas? What about the interests of the metropolitan area as a whole? Or of the region, the state, and the nation? How about other community interests, such as developers and builders; do they not have a right to be heard in the land-use decision-making process? How about the lower-income residents of the city who would like to move to the suburbs? How about modestly paid suburban workers who are excluded from suburban homes because of citizens association-backed plans and land-use ordinances? What of the interests of future generations?

There is no evidence that citizens associations are representing all of these interests; it is questionable whether they can or should be expected to. Changes in the substance of land-use control policy and in the character of land-use and planning decision-making processes are in order, changes that will broaden the horizons of land-use policy and widen the range of interests represented in the land-use decision-making process. Neither citizens groups nor any other single interest, such as builders or developers, should have the exclusive say.

NOTES

1. Civic associations are discussed in Edward C. Banfield and James Q. Wilson, City Politics (Cambridge, Mass.: Harvard University Press, 1963), chap. 17; and Herbert Kaufman, Politics and Policies in State and Local Governments (Englewood Cliffs, N.J.: Prentice-Hall, 1963), pp. 83-84.

2. Thomas R. Dye, Politics in States and Communities (Englewood Cliffs, N.J.: Prentice-Hall, 1969), pp. 249-50.

3. The Community Builders Handbook, Urban Land Institute (Washington, D.C.: The Institute, 1968), pp. 195-205.

4. William H. Whyte, The Last Landscape (Garden City, N.Y.: Doubleday, 1968), p. 235.

5. For insights into Alinsky's philosophy of community organization, see Marion K. Sanders, The Professional Radical: Conservations with Saul Alinsky (New York: Harper & Row, 1970).

6. See, for instance, Milton Kotler, Neighborhood Government (Indianapolis: Bobbs-Merrill, 1969); and Alan A. Altshuler, Community Control (New York: Pegasus, Western Publishing Co., 1970).

7. See, for example, James Q. Wilson, "Planning and Politics: Citizen Participation in Urban Renewal," Journal of the American Institute of Planners, November 1963, pp. 242-49.

8. Saul D. Alinsky, "Community Involvement in Deprived Neighborhoods," in Education and Manpower Strategies and Programs for Deprived Urban Neighborhoods, National League of Cities (Washington, D.C.: U.S. Office of Education, 1968), pp. 114-22.

9. Harmon Zeigler, Interest Groups in American Society (Englewood Cliffs, N.J.: Prentice-Hall, 1964), p. 30.

10. William Ebenstein, et al., American Democracy in World Perspective, 2d ed. (New York: Harper & Row, 1970), p. 306.

11. Interest groups are defined, fully discussed, and comprehensively analyzed in David B. Truman, The Governmental Process: Political Interests and Public Opinion, 2d ed. (New York: Alfred A. Knopf, 1971). Truman is the dean of contemporary interest group scholars. An earlier contributor to the interest group literature was Arthur F. Bentley; see his Process of Government (Chicago: University of Chicago Press, 1908).

12. Leo F. Schnore, "Metropolitan Growth and Decentralization," in William M. Dobriner, ed., The Suburban Community (New York: Putnam's, 1958), pp. 3-20.

13. Scott Greer, Governing the Metropolis (New York: John Wiley, 1962), pp. 94-95.

14. See Roscoe C. Martin, Government and the Suburban School (Syracuse, N.Y.: Syracuse University Press, 1962), p. 99. Martin observes: "It is not without significance that the PTA is more amenable . . . to bureaucratic influence than would be a continuing general-purpose organization comprising a cross-section of the community."

15. The ideal role of the planning agency in sewer (and other utility) programming is discussed in: William I. Goodman and Eric C. Freund, eds., Principles and Practice of Urban Planning (Washington, D.C.: International City Management Association, 1968), pp. 238-39.

16. The best-known study of this variety is Floyd Hunter, Community Power Structure (Chapel Hill: University of North Carolina Press, 1953); the setting for the study was Atlanta, Georgia. See also E. Digby Baltzell, Philadelphia Gentlemen (New York: The Free Press, 1958).

17. See Robert A. Dahl, Who Governs? Democracy and Power in an American City (New Haven, Conn.: Yale University Press, 1961); this is a study of New Haven, Connecticut. See also Roscoe C. Martin, et al., Decisions in Syracuse (Bloomington: Indiana University Press, 1961).

18. Seymour Martin Lipset, Political Man (Garden City, N.Y.: Doubleday, 1960), pp. 21-22.

19. Wallace S. Sayre and Herbert Kaufman, Governing New York City (New York: Russell Sage Foundation, 1960), pp. 481-82.

20. This study was conducted by Edwin E. Olson and Don T. Allensworth, with the assistance of Deborah Nager. The interviews took place in 1965, under the auspices of the University of Pennsylvania. This is the first publication of the study results.

6

**DIRECTIONS FOR
THE FUTURE**

This book has had a single goal: to demonstrate the need for planning and community development policy that provides for variety, diversity, experimentation, and opportunity. Too often master plans, zoning ordinances, subdivision regulations, and building codes have served to inhibit and prevent growth, change, and progress. The job at hand is to turn this policy around and get on with the task of building a better urban America.

In Chapter 2 we found that plans were frequently too specific in content and founded on the narrow ends of small communities and individual neighborhoods. This is not to suggest that every evidence of specificity in plans is undesirable or that the legitimate interests of neighborhoods and small jurisdictions should be denied representation in the planning process. It is reasonable to argue, however, that plans should be more general than they have been in the past and that they at least should be based on community-wide needs, alert public officials to future community facility needs, provide for needed future shopping and commercial sites, and set aside land for the future housing of all segments of society.

In Chapter 3 we noted that zoning may discourage development and that zoning may be used for exclusionary ends. Neither antidevelopment zoning, pure and simple, nor exclusionary zoning can be sustained if we are to meet pressing metropolitan needs for housing, commercial, and other urban land uses.

In Chapter 4 we discussed the weaknesses of the land-use and building control policies that affect housing and considered some of the ways by which these policies might be restructured. And in Chapter 5 we focused on citizens associations and their influence over community planning and land-use policy. Throughout, we have considered the actions that can be taken by the federal government and metropolitan institutions to effect needed changes in local planning and development policy. But the real challenge is in the local community. It is at the local level that change will have to take place; it is in the communities that the directions for the future will have to be charted. Let us then detail some steps that can be taken to improve the quality of community planning and development policy. After reviewing certain proposed substantive and administrative changes, we shall discuss actions that may be instrumental in effecting these measures.

NEW APPROACHES

Site Plans

Site plans were mentioned briefly in Chapters 1 and 3. Site plans now play an important role in some communities' planning processes. Normally, site plans are limited to commercial and mixed commercial-residential developments. Site plans are prepared by developers and commonly are reviewed by planning staffs and planning boards. Final approval of site plans often rests with the planning board.

Under conventional subdivision regulations, developers prepare subdivision plans that show the proposed road scheme, the proposed lot layout pattern, and other matters; these plans go through a preliminary and final stage and are subject to the review and approval of the planning board. Subdivision regulations were designed mainly for residential developments.

Site plans have a wider use than plans developed under conventional subdivision regulations. Site plans have considerable applicability to the type of development policy proposed in this study--that is, to policy calling for varied land uses and mixed population densities. Site plans are more detailed and cover more aspects of development than subdivision plans. They document the use of public space, for example, and go into such matters as building height. Nothing of planning significance is omitted. Legal provisions governing site plans are more general than typical subdivision regulations and permit more administrative discretion.

The use of site plans moves communities away from reliance on rigid land-use controls that permit little flexibility in development styles. It also shifts the burden of planning decision-making from zoning and other ordinances to the administrative sphere. The site plan process, of course, should include appropriate legal safeguards, but these can be couched in terms of performance standards rather than substantive prohibitions and restrictions. Proposed developments, considered under the site plan process, should meet generally accepted standards of safety, convenience, aesthetics, health, and community welfare; and this should be stated in the law. But detailed stipulations in community and state ordinances and legislation are not necessary and could significantly inhibit the potential contribution that the site plan process can make to community planning.

Local planning staffs and boards should have a voice in the review of site plans, but the present procedures in this area should be changed. The ultimate approval of site plans should not rest with local planners, or even with the local governing body, but with a group of experts who could evaluate these plans from the standpoint of a variety of professional perspectives. This group, which would have other duties, would be a "court of ecology."

The court of ecology would be part of the state government. Separate courts would be established at the state and local levels, although local courts would be part of the state system. A supreme court of ecology would be created for the state as a whole, and circuit courts of ecology for different districts in the state; the former would have appellate jurisdiction. The court of ecology is discussed further below.

The site plan process could be used for all types of proposed developments, including the residential variety. Although it has been used essentially for the consideration of commercial projects in the past, there is no reason why the site plan review process cannot be widened in scope in the future. It is particularly useful for considering large-scale developments that include several different land uses.

Contract Zoning

Contract, or conditional, zoning is based on the same principles as the site plan process. The objective is to introduce more flexibility into community development practices in order to promote greater efficiency in community living and working patterns.

Under contract zoning, as defined here, certain areas would be marked on the zoning map for unspecified or quite broad uses, or for uses subject to the approval of community planning authorities. Developers would propose uses and submit plans, maps, and models depicting the proposed uses. Public officials would consider the developer's proposal, agree with the developer on a mutually acceptable development plan, and contract with the developer to assure execution of the proposed plan. Governmental approval of the development package would be conditioned on the developer carrying out the agreed upon plan.

The site plan approach is generally preferable to contract zoning. One reason is that it probably would be easier to effect and more likely to encounter fewer legal obstacles. But contract zoning is a feasible alternative to the site plan. Again, final approvals under contract zoning should be made by the court of ecology, although the contract should be between the local governing body or planning board and the developer. Both the planning board and the local governing body should have a voice in contract zoning. A modified version of contract zoning is presently in effect in some communities.

Both the site plan and contract zoning approaches represent a departure from conventional zoning and subdivision control practice. Under both it is assumed that detailed public controls, lot by lot, tract by tract, would give way to more general and more effective control. The public interest is protected, and both public and private discretion is expanded. Because this constitutes a relatively new concept, the old process of public consideration of development proposals needs to be modified. The new process will be a stronger one.

New Zoning Categories

More specific substantive changes that can be made in community planning and zoning policy include the use of new zoning categories, namely planned unit development, new town, cluster, and vertical zoning. Traditionally, communities have been divided into separate districts and zoning categories have been applied to each district to assure segregation of land uses. Although the number of such categories typically has expanded beyond the early three (resi-

dential, commercial, industrial), most communities permit
little or no mixing of land uses within the same area;
this is particularly so in single-family residential neighborhoods.

Planned unit development, new town, cluster, and vertical zoning are designed to promote diversity and at
least some mixture of uses or housing patterns. Planned
unit development zoning is well-suited to large-scale undertakings. Where this category is applied, the developer is
free of customary constraints in the zoning ordinance, and
may vary lot sizes, housing types, and land uses within
general guidelines. Like the site plan and contract zoning
processes, planned unit development zoning shifts development determinations from the ordinance to administrators.
General conditions applying to planned unit development
zoning would include consistency with the community master
plan, compatibility with existing and planned community
facilities, and perhaps population density controls.

New town zoning is planned unit development zoning on
a broader geographical scale. New towns, which at present
may or may not be developed through new town zoning, can
be built for populations ranging up to 100,000 or more.
New town zoning typically permits considerable administrative
discretion and allows wide latitude in determining development styles and land uses.

Cluster zoning is a substantial advance over traditional residential zoning practices. Under cluster zoning,
homes in residential developments can be grouped without
regard to conventional lot size and setback requirements,
so long as the overall density is not changed. In a hun-
dred-acre tract, for example, conventional zoning may impose
a one-acre minimum lot size along with front-, back-, and
side-yard setback requirements. A developer theoretically
can build one house to the acre, up to a maximum of 100
houses. With cluster zoning, houses can be clustered without regard for conventional lot size and yard requirements,
and the area thereby "saved" can be reserved for open spaces
or other community uses.

The advantages of cluster zoning are that more efficient layout and design patterns can be effected, development and public improvement costs can be lowered, housing
prices can be cut, and much land can be put to common use.
In effect, the area presently so commonly included in large
lots and wide front, side, and back yards can be converted
into major areas of open space, common greens, and recreational, school, and other community uses. Previously in-
efficiently allocated private land is converted to public
use. Cluster zoning is sometimes called density zoning.

Under this concept several different centers, or clusters, of homes may be found in the same subdivision. Community facilities and recreational uses can be planned around these centers. Different methods can be used to manage community space provided under cluster zoning. School and park sites might be deeded to the local government, while certain open space and recreational areas might be given to a subdivision homeowners association. Cluster development is becoming more common, and it has gained widespread acceptance among planning boards, professional planners, and developers.

Vertical zoning provides for different uses in a single building. The basic zoning category involved in the vertical zoning concept may be commercial or high-density residential, but the idea is that apartments, shops, and offices (or any two of these) are permitted, stratified in the same structure. Vertical zoning is a new zoning practice in the suburbs; it is a step toward greater mixture of uses in outlying areas.

New Directions in Community
Development Ordinances
and Policy

In general, it is important to go beyond the traditional zoning and land-use control practices. Zoning and land-use regulations should be tools that facilitate development and at the same time protect the community interest. The conventional prohibitive and negative nature of zoning has not served the community interest, and it has inhibited originality and innovation in design and development. Planning can do much to discourage the continuation of old practices that are not serving broad community ends. Both planning and zoning should be positive, growth-minded, and progressive in character.

More flexibility should be introduced into community development policies. How this can be done is detailed in other parts of the book. Current community development policy is often too rigid, and this includes plans containing detailed specifications, zoning with high minimum lot-size and setback requirements, and building codes prohibiting the use of economical construction techniques. New zoning provisions calling for the construction of housing for low- and moderate-income groups should be general and not too specific. The imposition of rigid and inflexible requirements and burdens on developers will drive development from the community.

In adopting new zoning and land-use control practices, communities generally should develop their own procedures, ordinances, and codes. This will require a study of local conditions and the tailoring of legal provisions and regulations to meet these conditions. Although model ordinances and codes and neighboring jurisdiction practices should be studied, they should serve only as guides. If change in local land-use control policy requires new state legislation, so does change in state laws. The local input into new land development control practices is at least as important as the provisions of model laws or the laws of a neighboring jurisdiction; it may be more so.

NEW STRUCTURES

Two new types of structures would help promote new planning and development policy and would permit localities to better advance the public interest in community development. The most important of these is the court of ecology mentioned above. The other is metropolitan government.

Court of Ecology

The court of ecology would be a quasi-judicial agency, and it would be part of state government. It would have the power to review all basic community-level planning and land-use control decisions. It could be given power over other local and state decisions that impact significantly on community development. Community planning and land-use control decision-making processes would remain undisturbed, but the court of ecology would constitute another level above these processes. The court could consider community planning and land-use control decisions that are brought to it by concerned parties; it could uphold or overturn local decisions.

As noted, two levels would be included: a circuit court of ecology and a supreme court of ecology. The latter normally would consider questions on appeal from the former. In a typical state, several circuit courts of ecology would be created--one for each major subdistrict of the state. In most instances the decision of the circuit court would be final.

The court of ecology would be composed of professionals from various walks of life--including lawyers, architects, engineers, hydrologists, geologists, urbanologists, conservationists, and planners. The court would be given

the statutory duty of controlling the environment in the
public interest, and in its decisions it would consider
not only the interests of local communities and neighborhoods but also the metropolitan area and the state as a
whole.

The present state judiciary would still consider community development matters, but only those involving a constitutional question. Decisions of the court of ecology
could be taken to the state judiciary, but this would not
likely be normal procedure.

Normally, the ecology court system could be established
within the laws of a single state. State legislation would
create courts of ecology, spell out their powers, determine
their composition and the qualifications of their members,
and provide for their organization. In metropolitan areas
that cross state boundaries, special interstate ecology
courts could be created. These courts would be created by
interstate compact, as are water resources, mass transportation, and other agencies at present.

The appointment process would be determined by each
state on the basis of its own tradition and present views,
but it would seem logical that the governor would serve as
the appointing officer. If the governor selects members of
the ecology courts, he should do this in the light of
recommendations from the affected municipalities and counties and, perhaps, with the consent of the upper house of
the state legislature. The affected municipalities and
counties (in an area covered by a given circuit court of
ecology) could constitute a single unit for appointee recommendations (as a precedent, "city selection committees,"
composed of mayors of incorporated communities, make appointments to the San Francisco Bay Area Rapid Transit District
board).

Metropolitan Government

We have not been particularly sanguine about the prospects of achieving metropolitan government. Yet it seems
that metropolitan government holds some promise for some
parts of the country, and that a certain type of metropolitan government can be established without disturbing the
basic interests of local communities.

Metropolitan government refers to a single municipal
type of government serving the entire metropolitan area.
It may exist with or without subordinate local governments
(in all cases of metropolitan government to date, local

150

governments remain in existence). A county government normally is not considered a metropolitan government, even if
it serves the entire metropolitan area, because counties
frequently do not have municipal types of government.

There are two basic means of achieving metropolitan
government: federation and consolidation. Under federation, two levels of government are used; under consolidation,
the major general-purpose governments of the area are
merged into one unit. Consolidation usually means the merging of the central city government and the county government serving the area in and surrounding the central city;
theoretically, consolidation could mean the merging of all
governments in the metropolitan area into one. Metropolitan federation is probably best for most areas.

There are currently three metropolitan federations on
the North American continent: Miami-Dade County in Florida,
and Toronto and Winnipeg in Canada. In all three areas,
governmental powers are divided between central and local
governments. The central government has authority over the
metropolitan area as a whole and generally handles areawide
matters, while local or municipal governments have control
over local matters.

In Miami, officers are selected independently for
local and areawide posts. Yet the two levels are interre-
lated in important ways. The metropolitan government, for
example, sets minimum service standards that are to be met
by the municipalities. Metropolitan government responsibilities in Miami include urban renewal, housing, water supply,
parks and recreation, air pollution control, expressway
construction, and mass transit. In the community development area, metropolitanwide planning is a function of the
central government, although the basic zoning decision-
making authority rests with the municipalities, which number
over 25. The central government has the power to adopt
zoning and subdivision regulations for the entire metropolitan area; to date, it has enacted a uniform subdivision
ordinance that applies to undeveloped land throughout the
metropolitan area. The metropolitan government has adopted
an areawide land-use plan.[1]

In metropolitan Toronto, powers are divided between
the areawide government and six municipal governments.
Metropolitan government functions include arterial highways,
metropolitan parks, water supply, sewage disposal, and housing; municipal functions include police and fire protection,
local streets, and local parks. Areawide planning is a
responsibility of the metropolitan government, while local
planning and zoning are in the hands of municipal authorities.

Unlike the situation in Miami, members of the metropolitan governing board (called a council) represent municipalities and are not selected independently. In Greater Winnipeg, the metropolitan government has somewhat limited responsibilities; the metropolitan government may undertake planning for major roads, while basic general planning powers are found at the municipal level.[2]

Metropolitan government has been effected through consolidation in Baton Rouge, Louisiana; Nashville, Tennessee; Jacksonville, Florida; and Indianapolis, Indiana. In each case, the consolidation was a merger of the central city and county governments, with only one city and one county involved. The Jacksonville and Indianapolis consolidations took place within the past few years. Additional city-county consolidations occurred earlier in the country's history.

Under metropolitan government, it is more likely that broader considerations will be brought to bear on community planning and development processes than is the case under typical present arrangements. With the federation approach, local interests are protected through local government, but metropolitanwide interests also become inputs into the decision-making processes. It is appropriate that areawide planning be a responsibility of a metropolitan government, and zoning a function of local and municipal units. Communities would be expected to work within metropolitanwide guidelines and goals in setting local development policies. No specific metropolitan government plan is advanced here, as this is a matter for local determination.

ACTIONS NEEDED

A number of the participants in the community planning and development processes will have to act, and decisively so, if we are to effect new policies and administrative arrangements. Obviously, not all will agree on what needs to be done, and fewer on how to do it. But the general goal as presented in this study is clear, and there is likely to be considerable sympathy with it.

The cooperation of local and community forces will be vital. Professional planners, a number of planning board representatives, many developers, and progressive-minded community organizations have advanced many of the views presented here. These groups can be expected to work for the kinds of changes proposed.

States will have to act too. Some of the changes discussed will require new state legislation as well as amend-

ments to community ordinances. The states would play the
major role in the development of courts of ecology and in
the shaping of new metropolitan institutions. State governments can enact laws creating metropolitan governments,
and states can make it easier for communities to approve
such governments. No major planning or direct zoning effort,
however, is proposed for the states.

The federal government can help. As has been pointed
out, the national government has a number of grant and
other assistance programs in such areas as urban planning,
water facilities, sewers, housing, and urban renewal.
These programs are made available to local governments
among others. The federal government has a responsibility
to the public to see to it that these programs are used to
advance the broad interests of the community, the broad interests of the metropolitan area. These programs should
serve general ends, not narrow or parochial interests. It
is not easy to distinguish between broad or general and
narrow or parochial interests, but a better attempt should
be made.

Local authorities that use their planning and zoning
powers for exclusionary ends, that reject those methods designed to provide mixture, variety, and economy in housing
and development approaches, and that do not consider the
needs of the metropolitan area as a whole for commercial
and housing sites cannot be using federal grant and other
assistance for general purposes. For such communities,
federal programs should be the vehicle for promoting needed
change.

This is not to suggest that the federal government
should undertake to rule communities in planning, zoning,
or any other functional area that is properly a local matter.
Nor should federal assistance be arbitrarily or systematically withdrawn from localities, regardless of local conditions. And federal power should clearly not be used to attain political ends or to advance political aspirations.
These are dangers, and such tactics cannot be condoned, but
a reasonable and restrained use of federal powers to promote
better community development policy is entirely appropriate.

Federal money should not be used to underwrite or sus-
tain local planning and land-use policies that are economically discriminatory. These would include provisions of
plans that have the effect of excluding certain economic
classes, and zoning and other land-use practices that work
against the interests of one or more economic groups. This
is not to say that all communities must open their doors
to all income groups, but only that communities refrain from
using public authority to bar new residents on economic

153

grounds. The federal government can be highly instrumental in implementing this concept; it has seldom done so to date.

Federal money should not be used to facilitate local planning and land-use policies that exclude needed business uses. Federal authority should be tapped to encourage planning and zoning practices that provide for both commercial and different residential uses. Communities commonly have a need for new shopping and work areas as well as residential areas.

CONCLUDING NOTE

The plan for this study was conceived at a time when urban problem-solving has been highlighted as it never has been before. A number of approaches toward the solution of urban problems were launched in the 1960s, including the ill-fated community action programs and model cities, to name two. The study has tried to concentrate on those ideas and concepts that have the greatest potential for improving urban development patterns.

We do not wish to imply that all community development policies must be changed. There is much that is right about urban development; but there is much that is not. The study has focused on the latter. We can do much better than we have in the past. It is not too late.

NOTES

1. This paragraph is based largely on John C. Bollens and Henry J. Schmandt, The Metropolis, 2d ed. (New York: Harper & Row, 1970), pp. 327-35; and Building the American City, National Commission on Urban Problems (Washington, D.C.: Government Printing Office, 1968), p. 209.

2. Hugh L. LeBlanc and Don Trudeau Allensworth, The Politics of States and Urban Communities (New York: Harper & Row, 1971), pp. 241-42.

EPILOGUE:
WHY STATE PLANNING
WON'T WORK

Since this study was undertaken, much has been made of state planning. It has become "the thing." This epilogue is not written as a defense of the recommendations and conclusions of the study but to relate state planning to some of the concepts and insights presented in it. The study considered state planning as an alternative to present planning and land-use control administration patterns, and rejected it. The reasons for this are advanced in the following paragraphs.

Much of the current emphasis on state planning appears to have stemmed from two developments: (1) the State of Vermont's enactment of a general planning law in 1970 and (2) Senator Henry Jackson's land-use bill, first considered in the 91st Congress (1969-70). In addition, the administration introduced a national land-use policy act in 1971, and this played a role in the matter as well. Both the Jackson and administration proposals are designed to thrust the states into the planning and land-use process--and prominently so. The Jackson bill, for instance, would provide federal grants to the states to do statewide land-use planning and includes sanctions (cut-off of current federal aid) for states not undertaking such planning. The administration measure similarly calls for the states to develop land-use planning that would include the designation of areas of critical environmental concern and public facility impact, and to develop policies and methods for exercising control over such areas.[1]

State planning has gained momentum through the efforts of different professional organizations and public interest groups such as the Council of State Governments and the National Governors' Conference. Although the movement has only limited popular backing, it is generally supported by some key private groups, including such divergent interests as environmentalists, developers, builders, and organized labor. Of course not all developers, builders, or the others named are in this camp, and some real estate groups at the local level, for example, are strongly opposed to any transfer of planning power to the states. Since planning and zoning are currently local responsibilities, any significant involvement of the states in this area is bound to curtail local power.

155

It should be noted that only a few short years ago
most professional planners, planning administrators, important interest groups with stakes in planning, and others interested in the subject saw metropolitan and regional institutions as the answer to our planning woes. That local
planning was not working as it should seemed clear to most
then as now, but then the most commonly suggested alternative was metropolitan rather than state government. In
the mid-1960s, for instance, the Johnson administration
successfully pressed Congress for legislation favorable to
regional councils of governments, organized on a metropolitanwide basis. It was believed that purely local planning
was not enough and that the metropolitan perspective was
needed. And at the metropolitan level it was determined
that metropolitan planning commissions were not doing the
job, so councils of governments were tapped.[2] This reflected administration thinking at the time, but the idea
originally came from professionals in the field.

It should be noted that councils of governments differ
from metropolitan planning commissions in that they are
composed of elected local officials, while the latter generally are made up of appointed local officials, citizens,
and local planning board members. It was argued that since
elected officials have the final planning, zoning, and general development powers they should have the real control
at the metropolitan level as well. This was the next best
thing to full-fledged metropolitan governments directed
by their own elected officials (which few metropolitan areas
had then or have now). Metropolitan planning commissions
were first funded by the federal government in legislation
enacted in 1954 (making them all the more attractive to localities), but by the mid-1960s optimism about them had
waned, and the stock of councils of governments was up.

Specifically, the Housing and Urban Development Act
of 1965 authorized federal grants to "organizations composed
of public officials . . . representative of the political
jurisdictions" in metropolitan areas to undertake regional
planning programs. In addition, the Demonstration Cities
and Metropolitan Development Act of 1966 provided metropolitan areawide agencies responsible for metropolitan
planning with review power over certain federal grant and
loan applications submitted by local governments; these
agencies were "to the greatest extent practicable" to be
composed of and responsible to local elected officials.
Both of these measures were designed to extend federal
backing to councils of governments operating on a metropolitanwide scale and signified a withdrawal of some federal

support from planning commissions. Equally important was
that these measures represented a new emphasis on "metro-
politanism" in federal policy, and that this time the legislation had "teeth" (elected officials). With these laws,
especially with the prospect of federal money, councils of
governments proliferated; and one metropolitan area after
another added these councils to their existing local bodies
or "converted" their metropolitan planning commissions into
councils of government.

The election of the Republicans in 1968 may have had
something to do with changing all of this, although it is
as likely that the actions of the GOP were simply the sur-
face manifestations of a broader effort mounted by the
state public interest groups and some professional organizations. In any event, the new administration made no
secret of the fact that it leaned to the states when there
was a choice. In fact there often was a choice, since decisions had to be made in different grant programs as to
whether Washington would deal directly with the cities and
bypass the states (direct federalism) or work through the
states (which would then redistribute the funds to cities).[3]

Traditionally, the Democrats have lined up on the side
of localities and used their majorities in Congress to have
grants allocated directly to cities. Of course the Democratic base has been in the cities, and this strategy
therefore makes political sense. As early as the 1940s, a
Democratic city versus Republican state alignment appeared.
Shortly after World War II, for example, airport legislation
was held up for a year because the two parties could not
agree. The Democrats ultimately won this battle, and airport grants to this day are sent directly to cities. In
their stands both parties have had the backing of important
interest groups: the Democrats, that of the "city lobby"
including the National League of Cities and U.S. Conference
of Mayors; and the GOP, the state interest groups already
mentioned.[4] The Republicans, incidentally, are also politically motivated in taking their stand, as they have generally done better in the states than the cities.

That change was in the wind could be seen from Congress' enactment of crime control legislation in the late
1960s, in which Republicans and Southern Democrats outvoted
Northern liberals and directed that urban crime-fighting
money be funneled through the states (via bloc grants, a
new feature). This pattern disturbed the cities greatly,
and in a private survey municipal leaders questioned
whether the states would turn over the funds due them.
The cities have always argued that routing federal grants

destined for localities through the states was an unnecessary, wasteful, and perhaps risky step.

In the early 1970s, conference after conference was held stressing the need to shift planning and related responsibilities to the states. Some real estate interests were among the first to press the issue, especially the larger development and building firms that felt constrained by restrictive local regulations and whose political spokesman was the Council of Housing Producers.

The position was reduced to writing. Elizabeth Haskell began publicizing the case for state planning (through work in the Journal of the American Institute of Planners and elsewhere) and others provided academic backing for the concept.[5] By that time (1971), Vermont had approved state site development controls, Senator Jackson had held hearings on his land-use bill, and the administration had introduced its own measure on the subject.

In the 92d Congress, the Senate passed the National Land Use Policy and Planning Assistance Act of 1972, which contained features of both the Jackson and administration bills, but the House failed to act on the measure.[6] The central purpose of this, like the other land-use bills, was to put the states in the planning business or, legally speaking, to provide the financial and other federal inducements to the states for taking up statewide planning. New legislation was introduced in 1973 and action is expected on this before the end of the 93d session.

Although the specifics are not clear, it seems most likely that the states will be encouraged by national legislation or independent pressures to pass laws authorizing not only the undertaking of planning but some sort of land-use control as well. It is clear that the states could do this legally as they possess the police power, which permits them to regulate activity to advance the health, safety, and general welfare of the people. This is a power, it should be reiterated, which, in land use, has been largely delegated to local governments up to now.

But the point is, what would planning mean without the power to implement? This is a lesson the communities learned fast, and there is no reason to assume the states would come to any other conclusion. Many communities seem to skip planning in reality and move directly into land-use control, especially zoning (see Chapter 3); then plans are brought in to justify zoning patterns as a kind of afterthought.

In fact, the states that have gotten into the land-use act appear already to be thinking along similar lines. In

Vermont, for example, the state apparently has done much
more in the way of controlling land use than in planning.
Although three plans were envisioned in its recent legisla-
tion--inventory of land uses, capability and development,
and land-use plans--no final plan has been adopted by the
state.[7] At the same time, Vermont is regulating land use
throughout its territory, or in those areas not covered by
local land-use controls.

In the few other states that have done anything to
speak of in planning, such as Hawaii and Alaska, every indication is that much more has been done in zoning than
planning. Hawaii first passed a statewide land-use measure
in 1961, and under this legislation the state divided its
land area into four kinds of district: urban, rural, agri-
cultrual, and conservation. While specific uses in urban
districts are determined by county zoning regulations, specific uses in the other three kinds of district are governed directly by state controls. It would appear, however,
that Hawaii has no adopted master plan for the state as a
whole, unless the zoning actions are construed as consti-
tuting a plan, or that planning (as distinct from zoning)
was all that important to them anyway. Instructively, the
Hawaii law was enacted less as a means of promoting general
planning objectives than as a way to keep prime agricultural
land from being urbanized; it was in this light that the
law was backed by key agribusinesses, corporate farms, and
large estates; they viewed state land-use regulation as
promoting their economic interests. This again parallels
the situation in localities where in many cases key interest groups have found zoning and planning to their liking--
that is, as a vehicle by which to advance their economic
ends. At the state level, however, it seems that on balance
business and agricultural interests have the greatest voice,
while in localities outside central cities citizens groups
have a greater say.[8]

In the main, however, state involvement even in land-
use control has been limited. Some states have land-use
regulation powers over specific areas such as land around
state buildings and institutional holdings, flood plains,
marsh- and wetlands, and shorelines. Kansas and Oklahoma,
for instance, have the authority to zone around capitol
buildings; and Wisconsin and Rhode Island have the power to
zone in flood plains. Delaware, Michigan, Minnesota, and
Massachusetts have laws permitting the regulation of coastal
areas and/or wetlands. In a highly publicized measure approved in 1971, the Coastal Zoning Law, the State of Delaware banned all new heavy industry from its land area bor-

dering the Delaware Bay and the Atlantic ocean. Other
states currently prominently mentioned as having some land-
use powers include Maine (1970 Site Selection Act), Virginia (Land Use Policy Act of 1972), Florida (Environmental
Land and Water Management Act of 1972), North Carolina,
California, and Oregon.[9]

There are two questions that should be posed at this
point: Can the states do the job of planning and land-use
control? Should they? The first is by far the more important. The list of states with active planning programs is
small indeed, and there is no information presently available that suggests it will grow appreciably. If states do
move into planning in a major way, some force, almost certainly outside the state government itself, will have to
propel the move. But is this the way to get into planning?
And even if it is, will the interest groups that back state
planning as an academic matter do anything about it in
practice? Will they lobby for state planning in one state
capitol after another, releasing their staffs to travel
about pressing the case? Will they back their cause with
money? Will they educate state legislators in planning and
land use? For how otherwise can action be taken--or have
any practical meaning? We have seen how complex a subject
planning and zoning is, and it appears unlikely that the
states can act decisively or meaningfully without considerably more knowledge than they presently have. Without
education, state planning laws are likely to be implemented
poorly or not at all.

There is another point that has a bearing on this matter: the political power of local governments in the states.
Although local governments are "creatures" of the state,
this tells little about their political independence or
clout. In fact, local governments and their lobbyists
carry much weight in state capitals, and their associations
(of municipalities, counties, mayors, townships) are often
found among the more influential interest groups in state
legislatures.[10] As a practical matter, can the states step
into an area that local governments will be guarding with
all the resources at their command? And local governments
will be supported by key private interests that are currently dependent on local planning and zoning arrangements
and that stand to lose politically or economically from a
shift in assignments. An example of this can be cited in
the 1973 session of the Maryland legislature, in which a
proposed state land-use planning bill was watered down substantially because of local pressures. This measure, originally calling for mandatory state controls over critical

areas, now provides for only an advisory state role (actual land-use powers are to remain in localities).

Federal support will be needed if the states are to undertake important planning and zoning programs. But, in terms of the politics of the situation, can the states count on this support, even with the passage of a federal law on the subject? Will the federal government, in the last analysis, be willing to back the states on planning regardless of the administration or the pressures of the moment? Experience provides a clue. State and local governments have discovered that the federal government's commitment clearly is related to the administration in power. The present administration, for example, has cut back key urban and state funding programs even though subnational authorities had counted on them while developing their own budgets, staffing patterns, and other plans. Even should this federal administration support state planning, will the next do the same, especially if it is Democratic? The answer is not clear; it is by no means certain that it will. Also, if the states begin to threaten local governments on the land-use question, the latter will lobby against them in Washington, seeking to cut off federal backing for state planning. The cities are much better organized for political purposes at the federal level than the states are, and there is little question that the cities will draw on their power if the states move too far in this field.

The second question is important too. Should the states get into planning and zoning in a major way? This raises some key issues. For example, what will this change in the way of the substance of decisions, or in the way of the pressures surrounding the decisions? As has already been noted in the text of this study, there is no assurance that anything will change, and the evidence suggests that policy modifications are unlikely. In the long run, the states are subject to the same political pressures as localities, and if planning is not working in local government then for the same reasons it will not work in the states. In fact, it may be worse under state assignment, since this is the level traditionally most easily influenced by narrow interest group pressure. But in the long haul, even this is not likely, for local groups currently powerful will eventually gain influence at the state level. It is possible, for instance, that citizens group power over planning and zoning could be curtailed somewhat in the short run with a shift in assignments to the state level; but in the long run citizens forces would no doubt have about as much influence as they have now.

161

Further, many people in the localities fear the loss of grass-roots control of a function as important to them as planning and zoning. A transfer of planning to the states would trigger such fears and lead to a great deal of misunderstanding in the mind of the public. The lieutenant governor of Maryland, an opponent of state control of land use and planning, recently wrote a blistering letter to the Washington Post (a supporter of state planning) in which he stated, "The prospect of having local zoning disputes settled by a state bureaucrat in Baltimore is abhorrent to me. . . ."[11] This represents the views of many, and these views are sincerely held.

State boundaries do not correspond to population settlement patterns nor do they satisfy any other standard that would permit planning along more rational geographical or political lines; for example, state boundaries rarely coincide with natural boundaries such as major watersheds or river basins, which sometimes are used for planning purposes. At the same time, states could be effective, perhaps in planning for rural areas.

Other arguments might be considered. As an illustration, have states generally contributed to planning at the local level? The facts available suggest not. The states have not been much of a positive force in guiding or assisting local governments in developing and implementing master plans. They have not been sensitive to the need to direct their own activities so as to accord with local master plans. Time and time again states have violated both the letter and spirit of community plans and on one occasion after another have subverted local goals and programs. The best examples of this can be found in the planning of highways. State roads agencies have been among the major obstacles to carrying out local planning. Frequently, state highway bureaucracies have the unilateral power to locate roads anywhere they please--anywhere, that is, within the broad confines of legislative authority. And they have used this power, sometimes ruthlessly overriding local sentiment and community governments. This power extends to constructing new state highways and to reconstructing or widening existing ones. In one large metropolitan area on the East Coast, a superhighway proposed by a state roads department has been bitterly opposed by local citizens and the local governing body; yet the state, which has the authority, is proceeding with the freeway even though it will run through an area designated on the local master plan as an open-space wedge.

In fact, one of the reasons for a key provision of the 1962 highway act was to curtail the power of freewheeling state highway commissions who were not coordinating their roads with local planning. This legislation required (in effect) all large cities and their suburbs to develop a "continuing comprehensive transportation planning process." This arrangement, which was to include representation of each metropolitan area's local governments and the state highway agency, was designed to assure coordination of highway planning (a state task) with comprehensive planning (a local responsibility). However, even this has not worked out as well as its supporters had hoped, and in some areas outlying suburbs and highway representatives already have ganged up and voted radial suburb-to-city freeways over the opposition of central core representatives. Currently, this process extends only to major transportation projects, and until it is applied to purely local (intra-suburban) roads, little progress can be expected under any conditions.

The states' record in other functional areas is scarcely better. Although state aid to urban mass transit is to be commended (about a dozen states provide this as-sistance), the states have done little to coordinate their own programs with urban mass transportation planning. State transportation and highway departments have shown limited regard for local transit operations and the need to coordinate state transportation with urban mass transit planning. In a recent hearing in one state, the state highway division engineer was asked if a particular road would be planned to accommodate traffic flows into and out of a parking facility near a proposed transit stop. He replied, "That's not my problem." Too often, it appears, the states have considered local plans and objectives to be outside of their purview; "let the localities worry about their own problems" has all too commonly been the attitude.

In the area of schools, state performance has been similar. And education is an area which the states are about to enter on what may be a massive scale. This is so because of recent court rulings requiring an equalization of school resources on a statewide basis; the courts have found that under local control poor areas often have been short-changed and wealthy areas more abundantly funded. Again, what the states have done so far in this area has not been impressive--that is, from a planning standpoint. In general, state boards of education have been insensitive to local school planning, let alone planning of the more comprehensive variety. State education agencies have not infrequently funded projects not related to community zoning

163

and land-use policies, expected future densities, current
development patterns, or existing master plans.

In short, the states have done little to promote local
planning, and their powers have in many instances been used
to undermine or circumvent local plans. While this may not
be deliberate, it is nevertheless true and has adverse effects. The states, in brief, have added considerably to
the confusion in localities over planning and zoning. There
is enough confusion now, and it is hard to believe that
there could be more; but it seems likely that there will
be if the states are given the wide-ranging authority in
the planning and land-use field as proposed.

In some respects, it is no wonder that the states
have had such effects on local planning, for they have had
only minimal success at best in coordinating their own
programs and agencies. This may be because of the large
number of agencies, many independent or semi-independent
of the governor, in the typical state administration; because of the many elected officials in most state executive
branches, who are often in charge of their own departments
independent of the governor; because so many state agencies
are run by autonomous boards and commission; because state
legislatures commonly meet so infrequently; or for other
reasons. But, whatever the reasons, the situation exists.
In spite of the publicity given them, recent efforts of
the states to revamp their administrative structures and
consolidate departments have had little effect, and the same
is true of the highly touted state "clearinghouses" set
up through federal pressure to centralize state decision-
making.

Current state planning and present state planning
departments are not effective either. A recent general study
of state planning reports that there is "little coordinated
control by states over even their own construction and capital facilities."[12] Yet state control is now being put
forth as the solution to the nation's planning problems.
State planning agencies have demonstrated precious little
in the way of concrete action. Although all states have
such agencies, many of them are scarcely more than the old
economic development departments that have long been part
of state government, and most of the rest have no power,
political base, or professional staff to speak of. They
usually seem to be manned by a handful of professionals
whose chief duty to date has been to distribute federal
planning grants to small communities (larger areas receive
the grants directly). It would appear that no state planning agency has developed and adopted a statewide compre-

hensive land-use plan, and none seems to be close to doing
so. And if such a plan were developed, it would in all
probability have to be with local input or based largely
if not wholly on local plans--which amounts to no change
at all. State legislative pressures, which are frequently
locally based, certainly would be in this direction. It
is apt to be some time before state planning agencies are
able to rival those in the bigger cities and suburbs; and
perhaps there is no need for them to do so.

A number of state legislatures, likely a majority of
them, currently are considering some form of legislation
that will strengthen the state's hand in planning and land-
use control. Most of the bills seem to require state planning and the development of state land-use controls for
"critical areas" or developments or some such designation;
these areas might include proposed new towns or major population clusters, key intersections or interchanges or other
public improvements with a regional impact, and sites of
special environmental concern such as large bodies of water,
river basins, coast lines, historic districts, and wildlife preserves. Basically, the states appear to be "gear-
ing up" for the passage of the national land-use act, expected in 1973 or 1974. This study suggests that the states
should move cautiously in this area and that expectations
not be raised too high in the event of legislative action.

In sum, state planning is not the answer. This is
not because there is something inherently wrong with state
planning (for there is not) or that the states should not
be encouraged to set up stronger planning agencies. It is
just that one should be aware of what is likely to come
from this level. Planning and zoning have traditionally
been local responsibilities. Nothing has happened to suggest that state planning and zoning will be any better.
The same political forces are operative at both levels.
The task ahead is to broaden the base of local planning.
The specifics have been provided in Chapter 6.

NOTES

1. Richard G. RuBino and William R. Wagner, The
States' Role in Land Resource Management (Lexington, Ky.:
Council of State Governments, 1972).

2. Melvin B. Mogulof, Governing Metropolitan Areas:
A Critical Review of Council of Governments and the Federal
Role (Washington, D.C.: Urban Institute, 1971).

3. Recent studies of federalism and intergovernmental
relations include Arthur W. Macmahon, Administering Federal-

ism in a Democracy (New York: Oxford University Press,
1972); and Michael D. Reagan, The New Federalism (New York:
Oxford University Press, 1972).

4. An analysis of the "city lobby" in Washington is
found in Suzanne Farkas, Urban Lobbying: Mayors in the
Federal Arena (New York: New York University Press, 1971).

5. Elizabeth Haskell, "New Directions in State Environmental Planning," Journal of the American Institute of
Planners, XXXVII, 4 (July 1971), 253-58; and Elizabeth H.
Haskell, Victoria Price, et al., Managing the Environment:
Nine States Look for New Answers (Washington, D.C.: Woodrow Wilson International Center for Scholars, 1971). See
also the report in Note 7 below.

6. U.S. Congress, Senate, Committee on Interior and
Insular Affairs, Report on Land Use Policy and Planning Assistance Act of 1972 to Accompany S. 632 (No. 92-869) (Washington, D.C.: Government Printing Office, 1972).

7. Fred Bosselman and David Callies, The Quiet Revo-
lution in Land Use Control (Washington, D.C.: Government
Printing Office, 1972), pp. 54-107. This provocative report was prepared for the Council on Environmental Quality,
a recently created federal agency and a strong advocate of
a broader state role in planning and land-use control.

8. Precise determinations of the power of different
interests in the states can be made only at great risk.
For a study of the interest groups perceived to be the most
powerful in four states, see Harmon Zeigler and Michael
Baer, Lobbying: Interaction and Influence in American State
Legislatures (Belmont, Calif.: Wadsworth Publishing Co.,
1969). Business groups were named among the most powerful
organizations in all of the states, and farm groups in
three of the four; citizens associations (neighborhood
variety) were listed in none of the states. Legislators
and lobbyists did the judging.

9. Environmental Quality, The Third Annual Report of
the Council on Environmental Quality (Washington, D.C.:
Government Printing Office, 1972), pp. 157-99.

10. One study, for example, found interest groups representing local governments to be influential in a number
of state legislatures, including Arkansas, Georgia, Pennsylvania, Wisconsin, and New York. This was based on the per-
ceptions of the state legislators themselves. Wayne L.
Francis, Legislative Issues in the Fifty States: A Comparative Analysis (Chicago: Rand McNally, 1967).

11. Washington Post, December 6, 1972, p. A-17.

12. John N. Kolesar, "The States and Urban Planning
and Development," in Alan K. Campbell, ed., The States and
the Urban Crisis (Englewood Cliffs, N.J.: Prentice-Hall,
1970), p. 131.

R. ROBERT LINOWES is among the more prominent zoning attorneys in the country. He has a successful law practice in Montgomery County, Maryland and Washington, D.C. He has served as zoning attorney for some of the largest developments on the East Coast as well as zoning attorney for municipalities and citizens groups. His firm, Linowes and Blocher, has represented the developers of a number of major office-shopping-residential complexes.

Mr. Linowes has been an innovator in developing new land-use concepts contributing to orderly development. Mr. Linowes served in the county attorney's office in Montgomery County and currently is advising the government of the District of Columbia on inner-city redevelopment.

Mr. Linowes has an L.L.B. from Columbia University and is a member of the American, Maryland, District of Columbia, and Montgomery County Bar Associations and the American Society of Planning Officials.

DON T. ALLENSWORTH (Ph.D.) is an author and lecturer in political science. He has written several books on American government and politics and has talked before public and private groups on the subject. At the college level, he has lectured on American politics, urban government, and city planning processes.

Dr. Allensworth is the author of the recently published U.S. Government in Action series, which includes the textbooks Policy and Structure, Public Policy and Political Change, and Essentials. In addition, he is coauthor of The Politics of States and Urban Communities, published in 1971.

Dr. Allensworth has been adviser to city planning agencies and local governments, has served as consultant to the National League of Cities, and has been a member of the governor's reorganization staff in Ohio. He has spoken before state legislators and federal and municipal administrators and has served as Visiting Lecturer in Political Science at the University of Pennsylvania, where he was affiliated with the faculty of the Fels Institute of Local and State Government.

THE IMPACT OF FEDERAL LEGISLATION AND PROGRAMS
ON PRIVATE LAND IN URBAN AND METROPOLITAN DEVELOPMENT

Joseph L. Stevens

COMMUNITY GROWTH AND WATER RESOURCES POLICY

John M. Carson
Goldie W. Rivkin
Malcolm D. Rivkin

MUNICIPAL DECENTRALIZATION
AND NEIGHBORHOOD RESOURCES:

Case Studies of Twelve Cities

George J. Washnis